John MacArthur

The divorce dilemma

Day One

dilemma

God's Last Word on Lasting Commitment

Unless otherwise stated, all Scripture quotations are taken from the **New American Standard Bible®**,
Copyright © 1960, 1962, 1963, 1968, 1971, 1972, 1973, 1975, 1977, 1995 by The Lockman Foundation
Used by permission. (www.lockman.org)

British Library Cataloguing in Publication Data available

ISBN 978–1–84625–107–8

Published by Day One Publications
Ryelands Road, Leominster, England, HR6 8NZ

☎ 01568 613 740
FAX: 01568 611 473
email—sales@dayone.co.uk
web site—www.dayone.co.uk

Day One Christian Ministries Inc
427 Wade Hampton Blvd
Greenville SC 29609 USA

☎ Toll free 888–329–6630

☎ 864–233–5374
FAX: 864–233–5376

Cover designed by Wayne McMaster and printed in the United States

I am profoundly grateful to Gerard and Philippa Chrispin for their hard work editing the original draft of this book. The volume you hold in your hands is a reality first of all because of Gerard's vision, and I'm deeply indebted to him for his encouragement and persistence throughout the process of getting the material prepared for publication.

Thanks also to Allacin Morimizu, without whose hard labor and sacrificial service the final draft might never have seen the light of day. The excellency and efficiency of her editorial skills are evident on every page of the book.

My special thanks go to Day One for their partnership, and for their patient commitment to this project.

1 In the beginning

T he many confusing and conflicting ideas in our day about Scripture's teaching on divorce are not caused by any lack of clarity or any other deficiency in God's revelation, but by the fact that sin has clouded men's minds to the straightforward simplicity of what God has said. When people read the Bible with the biases of their own preconceptions or fleshly appetites, a perplexing picture is the only possible outcome. The cause of so much confusion lies not with God but with the fallen sinfulness of the human race.

This book's title, *The Divorce Dilemma*, is a realistic description of our human confusion. The subtitle, *God's Last Word on Lasting Commitment*, is meant to underscore my confidence that God's Word is clear, and that He gives wisdom and understanding to those who humbly consider His Word.

We will systematically examine three key passages in the New Testament that directly address the topics of divorce, remarriage, and God's attainable ideal for marriage. Two of those passages are found in the Gospel of Matthew (chapters 5 and 19) and consist of words from our Lord's own lips; the third is direct revelation from God through the pen of the Apostle Paul in his first epistle to the Corinthians (chapter 7). We'll examine those texts and their contexts, and allow Scripture to shape our perspective on this difficult topic.

It's important to turn to Scripture for answers to our questions about divorce. Neither sentiment nor personal experience is a safe guide.

Churches are culpable

Unfortunately, many Christians have never really examined the issues of marriage, divorce, and remarriage *biblically*. Churches today often give few or wrong guidelines for marriage and divorce—or none at all. As a result, confusion abounds regarding these issues in the Christian community. Sometimes even the most basic biblical guidelines are ignored or overlooked.

I've seen this many times, firsthand. As a matter of fact, the first crisis I experienced in my ministry was when a leading family in the church where I was a young pastor asked me to officiate at the wedding of the daughter, a Christian, to a non-Christian man. I told them I couldn't do it. Believers are not to be unequally yoked with unbelievers (2 Corinthians 6:14), and if I married the couple I would be affirming and validating an act of disobedience to the clear teaching of Scripture. I would not knowingly do that.

At the time, our elders seemed uncertain of what to do, so we met to discuss it. Someone offered this suggestion: 'You don't have to do it if it's against your conscience, but the family wants the wedding to take place in their church. We can get someone else to perform the ceremony.'

I responded, 'This is not just a private matter of conscience. The Scriptures say it is wrong for a Christian to marry a non-Christian. It's wrong no matter who performs the ceremony. I can neither participate actively by performing the ceremony, nor give my consent passively by allowing someone else to officiate in my place.' Then I reminded the elders, 'This is Christ's church, not *our* church. We cannot consent to an act that dishonors Him while pretending to give our blessing as undershepherds charged with guarding the flock of God.' Looking at it that way, the elders of the church agreed. The decision was controversial for a brief time, but ever since that incident, our church has had a reputation for being a place where the Word of God is taken seriously.

Not all churches are willing to take a stand like that, however. Some churches and pastors will marry anybody to anybody under any circumstances. The topics of sex and relationships are often treated flippantly and casually from the pulpit, without the restraint and dignity seen in God's Word. Over the past half-century, Western society has become increasingly materialistic, selfish, and carnal—and so have many churches. As a consequence, faithful church leaders have to deal daily with a never-ending stream of problems associated with divorce because their people do not know how to sustain right relationships. The way for anyone to learn how is in the Word of God.

Four views on divorce

The Bible clearly teaches what God thinks about divorce: He hates it (Malachi 2:16), and so should we. The problem is that people are tempted to ignore the Bible's clear teaching because they want to justify what they want to do, so they try to find something in the Scriptures or elsewhere to support their desires. The diversity of opinions about marriage and remarriage, the growing tolerance of easy divorce, and the abundance of broken families in our culture are inevitable fruits of that attitude. Whenever people form their beliefs based on convenience and personal preference rather than listening to (and submitting to) what God's Word actually says, confusion reigns.

Still, there are fundamentally only four dominant views about divorce: First, secular society (and, sadly, even many professing Christians) would allow divorce and remarriage anytime, for anybody, for anything. In the historic evangelical mainstream (that community of Christians who profess to believe the Bible implicitly, take its standards seriously, and look to Christ alone for salvation), that view has never been the dominant one.

Instead, conservative pastors, Bible commentators, and theologians are generally divided among three other views: Second, some would insist that, biblically, there is to be no divorce at all for anybody, not for any reason, or under any circumstances. Third, others teach that divorce under certain circumstances is permissible but no remarriage is allowed—ever— at any time, for anybody, for any reason. And fourth, others say that, biblically, both divorce and remarriage are possible, but only under certain circumstances.

Which option is truly biblical? We find the answer in Jesus' Sermon on the Mount.

The Pharisees of Jesus' day

Like many people today, the Jewish leaders of Jesus' day, typified by the Pharisees, had developed their own standards for divorce and remarriage, but they presented them to the people as God's standards. In Matthew 5:31–32 we find Jesus setting the record straight: 'It was said, "Whoever sends his wife away, let him give her a certificate of divorce"; but I say to you that everyone who divorces his wife, except for the reason of unchastity, makes her commit adultery; and whoever marries a divorced woman commits adultery.'

Here is the context: Jesus was confronting the sins of the Pharisees, and He was unmasking their hypocrisy. He was showing how they exchanged God's standards for their own because they could not keep His. They dragged God down to their own level and invented their own code of ethics. Making matters worse, they misinterpreted the Bible to fit their own views. A majority of the Pharisees decided that any husband ought to be able to shed his wife whenever he wanted, so they twisted a Scripture passage to fit that wicked notion.

The passage they twisted was Deuteronomy 24:1–4, so that is where Jesus began His teaching on divorce and remarriage in order to lift the people out of the mud and onto God's high ground.

Our text in Jesus' Sermon on the Mount, Matthew 5:31–32, begins, 'It was said …' That does not refer to the Old Testament Law, but to what people had been wrongly taught by the rabbis. It is similar to verse 21, where we read that Jesus said, 'You have heard that the ancients were told …' In both cases He answered with, 'But I say to you …' He was declaring with authority, 'What you have heard is wrong, but what I am telling you is right.' In fact, when Jesus finished the Sermon on the Mount, 'The crowds were amazed at His teaching; for He was teaching them as one having authority [in and of Himself], and not as their scribes,' who quoted other people's authority (Matthew 7:28–29). Our Lord gave precise biblical teaching to correct the traditional misinterpretation that led to the people's misunderstanding about divorce.

The people, guided by their leaders, tolerated divorce and remarriage for any reason. Jesus' response in verse 32 is that God does not permit divorce, except for one very specific reason.

The exception clause is important. Notice that while Jesus was plainly confronting the Pharisees' too-lax attitude toward divorce, He expressly recognized an exception: 'except for the reason of unchastity.' As we shall see in an upcoming chapter, He was speaking of the kind of serious, unrepentant sexual sin that represents a full-on assault against the sanctity of the marriage union and irreparably fractures every vestige of trust and intimacy. In other words, it was supposed to be an uncommon exclusion to the prevailing rule, and always informed by the reality that God hates divorce.

Some Christians, with the good motive of wanting to halt the social ills of divorce, would prefer to ignore or explain away the exception clause and insist that divorce is never permissible, period. But we can't outthink Jesus and must not make the Law more rigid than He did. We need to deal honestly with *everything* He taught, and not add to or subtract from His Word. Let's explore further to see exactly what He said about divorce and why.

The certificate of divorce

The rabbinic justification for such easy divorce was based on an erroneous interpretation of Deuteronomy 24:1–4, the Bible's earliest mention of a certificate of divorce:

When a man takes a wife and marries her, and it happens that she finds no favor in his eyes because he has found some indecency in her, and he writes her a certificate of divorce and puts it in her hand and sends her out from his house, and she leaves his house and goes and becomes another man's wife, and if the latter husband turns against her and writes her a certificate of divorce and puts it in her hand and sends her out of his house, or if the latter husband dies who took her to be his wife, then her former husband who sent her away is not allowed to take her again to be his wife, since she has been defiled; for that is an abomination before the LORD, and you shall not bring sin on the land which the LORD your God gives you as an inheritance.

The focus of that passage is not whether divorce is permitted. It does not provide any explicit guidelines for when divorce might be allowable or not, much less *command* divorce in any instance. The point is that improper divorce leads to adultery, which results in defilement. Through Moses, God recognized and permitted divorce under certain circumstances, when it was accompanied by a certificate, but He did not thereby condone or command divorce. God's permission for divorce was an accommodation of His grace to human sin. 'Because of your hardness of heart,' Jesus explained to the Pharisees on another occasion, 'Moses permitted you to divorce your wives; but from the beginning it has not been this way' (Matthew 19:8).

The certificate did not make the divorce right, but only gave the woman some protection. It protected her reputation from slander and provided proof that her former husband divorced her.

A literal rendering of the Hebrew word translated 'indecency' in Deuteronomy 24:1 is 'the nakedness of a thing.' That encompasses every kind of improper, shameful, or indecent behavior unbecoming to a woman and embarrassing to her husband. It cannot refer to adultery because death was the penalty for that back then (Leviticus 20:10). What kind of indecency led to that certificate of divorce in Deuteronomy 24? It must have been a sin of unfaithfulness or promiscuity that stopped just short of actual adultery.

The Lord's primary purpose in Deuteronomy 24:1–4 was not to give an excuse for divorce but to show the potential evil of it. His intention was not to provide for it but to prevent it. Because the woman's divorce from her first marriage lacked sufficient ground, her second marriage would be adulterous. She was 'defiled,' which literally means 'disqualified' in the Hebrew text, because of the adultery brought about by her second marriage.

Moses' point was that unjustified divorce for 'indecency' proliferates adultery since remarriage usually follows on the heels of divorce. As a new pastor, I witnessed that reality when a woman at my church accused her husband of indecency because she didn't like his personal hygiene. He decided to divorce her and they both ended up marrying other people, all of whom in the process became adulterers in God's sight.

So from God's perspective, the granting of a certificate does not in itself make any divorce legitimate. Far from approving divorce, Deuteronomy 24:1–4 is a strong warning against it.

Back to the beginning

The Bible's teaching on divorce cannot be understood apart from its teaching on marriage. In Genesis 2:21–23 we read that God created first Adam and then Eve, putting them together in a wonderful union. Upon meeting his wife, awestruck Adam proclaimed, 'This is now bone of my bones, and flesh of my flesh; she shall be called Woman, because she was taken out of Man.' Verse 24 continues, 'For this reason a man shall leave his father and his mother, and be joined to his wife; and they shall become one flesh.' Marriage was God's plan, not man's. In the deepest sense, every couple that has ever been married participates in a union established by the Creator Himself. Marriage, therefore, is a divine institution.

From the beginning, God intended monogamous, lifelong marriage to be the only pattern of union between men and women. 'Joined to his wife' carries the idea of firm, permanent attachment, as in gluing. In marriage, a man and woman are so closely joined that they become 'one flesh.' God brings them together in a unique physical and spiritual bond that reaches to the very depths of their souls. Marriage is the welding of two people together into one unit, the blending of two minds, two wills, two sets of emotions, and two spirits. They are not two anymore: From a divine perception, a man and his wife are one, and one is an indivisible number. The Lord intends for that bond to be indissoluble as long as both partners are alive.

The goal is a perfect oneness, both in the intimacy of the physical and in the intimacy of the spiritual. Marriage is a sharing of those things in life that cannot be shared with any other human being. God created sex and procreation to be the physical expression of that oneness. If there is only the sexual union, however, and not a oneness of spirit through the commitment of marriage, then the physical act is meaningless, self-centered, and exploitative.

Adam and Eve were created to enjoy a blissful, loving, and caring relationship as husband and wife. In the Garden of Eden, Adam and Eve ruled together, with him as the head and her as his helper. God created man and woman equal in many ways, but He gave them clearly different roles. Adam's headship was a loving, caring, understanding provision of leadership. Eve's role was that of loving, willing submission and support. Both were totally devoted to the Lord and to each other. Theirs was a perfect, balanced, and majestic co-regency over all the earth (Genesis 1:27–28).

The first marriage problem

Genesis 3 describes the disastrous Fall of mankind. Notice how it affected marriage. Eve did not consult Adam, her head and protector, when confronted with temptation. She easily succumbed to Satan's wiles. When

Adam forfeited his role of headship and willingly followed her lead, he also fell victim to sin. That first sin brought a separation of God from man, a separation of man from nature, and a separation of husband from wife. The curse on Adam and every man after him was, 'Cursed is the ground because of you; in toil you will eat of it all the days of your life. Both thorns and thistles it shall grow for you' (Genesis 3:17–18). God's curse on Eve and all women after her was, 'I will greatly multiply your pain in childbirth, in pain you will bring forth children; yet your desire will be for your husband, and he will rule over you' (verse 16). The desire spoken of here does *not* refer to her original God-given desire for loving submission and companionship, which she already had before the Fall.

The Fall distorted and perverted the marriage relationship. Henceforth the wife's 'desire' for her husband would no longer be the desire to help but the desire to control—the same desire sin personified is described as having to influence Cain to murder his brother, Abel. Before the deed was done, God warned Cain, saying, 'Why are you angry? And why has your countenance fallen? If you do well, will not your countenance be lifted up? And if you do not do well, sin is crouching at the door; and its desire is for you, but you must master it' (Genesis 4:6–7). Both Genesis 3 and 4 describe wicked desires that seek to dominate against God's will.

For the man's part, his 'rule' over his wife would henceforth be one of stern control, an overly defensive reaction against her desire to control him. His rule over her would no longer be benevolent and selfless, as it was in the beginning, but overbearing and selfish. At the Fall the battle of the sexes began, and women's liberation and male chauvinism have ever since been clouding and corrupting God's original plan for marriage.

Treatment or amputation?

One of the most tragic consequences of that battle is the propensity to divorce. But in light of God's perfect plan for marriage—the plan followed but for a brief while in the Garden of Eden—it is clear that divorce is like a person cutting off an arm or leg because of a splinter in it. Instead of dealing with whatever trouble arises between husband and wife, divorce tries to solve the problem by destroying the union.

On an even deeper level, divorce destroys a union that God Himself has made. That is why Jesus said unequivocally, 'What therefore God has joined together, let no man separate [divorce, or put asunder]' (Matthew 19:6). Husbands and wives who realize that God has joined them into a single entity will not be so foolish as to hurt the other because they know they also hurt themselves. Therefore, when God brings a man and a woman together in marriage, theirs is to be a lifelong relationship. God, as its Creator, never wants anyone to sever that relationship. Divorce is a denial of His will and a destruction of His work.

Yet today, so many people simply walk away from marriage if they feel it is not working out the way they think it should. They are surprised when they see others working hard at their marriages, trying to remove the splinter rather than amputate the arm or leg, when it appears on the surface so much easier to move on and find someone else.

God's serious view of marriage

If we see marriage the way God sees it, we view it as a monogamous, lifelong oneness that He has designed. So sacred is marriage, so absolutely sacred is this oneness, that the penalty for violating it was death. The Seventh Commandment says, 'You shall not commit adultery' (Exodus 20:14). Adultery is sexual involvement with someone other than your spouse. Leviticus 20:10 says, 'If there is a man who commits adultery with another man's wife, one who commits adultery with his friend's wife, the adulterer and the adulteress shall surely be put to death.'

In those early years, when God was establishing the highest possible law for the instruction of man, God so hated anything that defiled marriage that the penalty was death. God's attitude toward marriage has not changed. Adultery is sexual activity with a married person. Fornication is sexual activity between unmarried people. God also considers that evil and sinful, but because it does not break an existing marital union, the prescribed punishment in Leviticus 19:20 was scourging, not death: 'If a man lies carnally with a woman … there shall be punishment; they shall not, however, be put to death …' This gives us some insight into how God feels about marriage.

Coveting and lusting

The last of the Ten Commandments also reflects God's high view of marriage: 'You shall not covet … your neighbor's wife' (Exodus 20:17).

God is stating that for a married person even to desire another partner is so evil that it is one of the ten major sins. Jesus reiterated that point in the Sermon on the Mount: 'I say to you that everyone who looks at a woman with lust for her has already committed adultery with her in his heart' (Matthew 5:28). Even to contemplate adultery is forbidden. This is how important an emphasis God places on faithfulness in marriage.

The Lord our God is so concerned about the sanctity of marriage that He instructed a variety of sensible precautions to be taken to avoid temptation. For example, Exodus 20:26 ordered that the altar of the Israelites was to be built on flat ground, rather than on high ground reached by steps, as the pagans had. That way, there could be no immodest exposure of anyone standing on the altar to whoever was standing below. That is a far cry from the way we conduct ourselves today. We should realize that when Adam and Eve sinned in the Garden, one of the first things the Lord did was cover them up (Genesis 3:21). All men and women are meant to be covered up because now sin has entered the world, temptation to impurity can be induced in many ways by how people dress. We need to be sensitive in those areas.

A step further

In Leviticus 18:18 God went a step further and forbade polygamy. He wants no one to have more than one partner. God established marriage as a spiritual, sexual, social union for one man and one woman never to be violated in thought or in deed. He condemned in a wholesale manner every violation of it and anything that could tempt a marriage partner to violate it. God's view of marriage is a monogamous, lifelong, permanent union between two people. It is an indivisible oneness. It is the will of God that we be committed to the uniqueness and permanence of marriage, with two becoming one for life.

Hypocrisy and treachery

God confirms his absolute hatred of divorce in Malachi 2:13–16:

'You cover the altar of the LORD with tears, with weeping and with groaning, because He no longer regards the offering or accepts it with favor from your hand. Yet you say, "For what reason?" Because the LORD has been a witness between you and the wife of your youth, against whom you have dealt treacherously, though she is your companion and your wife by covenant. But not one has done so who has a remnant of the Spirit ... Take heed then to your spirit, and let no one deal treacherously against the wife of your youth. For *I hate divorce,' says the* LORD, the God of Israel, 'and him who covers his garment with wrong,' says the LORD of hosts. 'So take heed to your spirit, that you do not deal treacherously' (emphasis added).

The man who breaks his lifetime vow to his wife does what God hates. (The same is true for a woman who breaks her lifetime vow to her husband.) He who does so 'covers his garment with wrong.' The literal rendering is 'covers his clothes with violence,' a vivid picture of a murderer stained with the blood of his victim. That is a sobering view of what divorce really does to you and the one to whom you pledged yourself for life before God and other witnesses. 'Not one has done so who has a remnant of the Spirit,' a difficult text in Hebrew, is essentially saying that God's Holy Spirit is never a party to divorce.

Many people today claim to be led by the Lord to get a divorce and to have His peace after they leave their spouses. God, however, continues to declare, 'I hate divorce ... So take heed to your spirit, that you do not deal treacherously.' Don't fool yourself; don't try to fool others. A lady came to me in church and said, 'My husband comes to church with me every week to keep up the façade, but all week long he is living with another woman.' What does God think about that man's worship? He has no regard for it. Why? Because that man is acting treacherously against the wife of his youth to whom he has been married over thirty years. God is not interested in his worship; it is a mockery. The wife of your youth 'is your companion,' says Malachi 2:14, using a beautiful Hebrew word that describes close friends in the Old Testament. This is the only place it is ever used for a wife, but it does indicate that your wife should be your closest friend. If she is not, ask yourself what you can do to change that. Share your life with her. Don't shut her out.

Divorce discouraged

Without exception, divorce is a product of sin, and God hates it. He never commands it, endorses it, or blesses it. Far from encouraging divorce, nearly all the references to divorce in the Old Testament put restrictions on it. For example, Deuteronomy says about a husband who falsely accuses his bride of 'shameful deeds' that 'they shall fine him a hundred shekels of silver and give it to the girl's father, because he publicly defamed a virgin of Israel. And she shall remain his wife; he cannot divorce her all his days' (22:14, 19). In the same chapter we read, 'If a man finds a girl who is a virgin, who is not engaged, and seizes her and lies with her and they are discovered, then the man who lay with her shall give to the girl's father fifty shekels of silver, and she shall become his wife because he has violated her; he cannot divorce her all his days' (verses 28–29).

When God instructed Moses on the purity of the priests, He went an extra measure to keep His priests from being even remotely tainted by divorce. This is what He said about the women eligible for a priest to marry: 'A widow, or a divorced woman, or one who is profaned by harlotry, these he may not take; but rather he is to marry a virgin of his own people, so that he will not profane his offspring among his people; for I am the LORD who sanctifies him' (Leviticus 21:14–15). God's priests were allowed to marry, but only in the purest of circumstances. Death, divorce, and harlotry are all great evils, and with divorce keeping such awful company, who would willingly choose it? The prophet Hosea did not, even when his wife became a harlot.

Amazingly patient love

The entire Book of Hosea is a picture of God's forgiving and patient love for Israel, dramatized by the prophet Hosea's forgiving and patient love for his wife, Gomer. Gomer prostituted herself, forsook Hosea, and was unfaithful to him in every possible way. The heart of the story is that Hosea was faithful and forgiving, just as God is faithful and forgiving. Poor Hosea's heart was broken when his wife indulged in wickedness, but he stayed close to the Lord, who sustained him. Marriage is *not* the key to happiness; God is. If you are right with God, He will help you to have right relationships with others.

Some people will still refuse you, but Hosea was successful in wooing back his bride with patient, sacrificial love. He met her needs during all the dark times, but also made it hard for her to continue in sin. I've known and admired men who have followed their unfaithful wives and spoken to their partners in adultery—even sometimes their employers—to help their wives say, as Gomer finally did, 'I will go back to my first husband, for it was better for me then than now!' (Hosea 2:7). The Book of Hosea concludes on the hopeful note of God's saying to His people, 'I will heal their apostasy, I will love them freely, for My anger has turned away from them' (14:4). This is how Hosea himself concluded the book bearing his name: 'Whoever is wise, let him understand these things; whoever is discerning, let him know them. For the ways of the LORD are right, and the righteous will walk in them, but transgressors will stumble in them' (14:9). Although Hosea and Gomer's marriage is primarily a symbol of God's relationship to His people Israel, it is also a practical illustration of how to deal with a wayward spouse.

God looks on the union of husband and wife in the same way He looks on the union of Himself with believers. Shouldn't the way of God be the way of His people—to love, forgive, draw back, and seek to restore the partner who is willing to be restored? Do we want God to cast us away when we're the ones doing the sinning—to treat us on a one-false-move-and-you're-done basis, as so many marriages are handled now?

Love that nourishes and cherishes

God's forgiving love seeks to hold the union together. That is how Christ loves His church, which is a model for every husband. Ephesians 5 explains,

Husbands, love your wives, just as Christ also loved the church and gave Himself up for her, so that He might sanctify her, having cleansed her by the washing of water with the word, that He might present to Himself the church in all her glory, having no spot or wrinkle or any such thing; but that she would be holy and blameless. So husbands ought also to love their own wives as their own bodies. He who loves his own wife loves himself; for no one ever hated his own flesh, but nourishes and cherishes it, just as Christ also does the church (verses 25–29).

The two key attitudes in a successful marriage are self-denial and self-giving, both of which are contrary to human nature but made possible to those who trust in God through Christ.

A related truth is the Golden Rule our Lord gave in the Sermon on the Mount: 'Treat people the same way you want them to treat you'

(Matthew 7:12). You'll never have a better opportunity to do that than in marriage. There must be forgiving love and restoring grace in a marriage. That alone makes marriage a proper symbol of God's forgiving love and restoring grace. That is the magnificence of marriage. Its permanence symbolizes God's permanent relationship with His people. To pursue divorce is to miss the whole point of God's dramatization in the story of Hosea and Gomer, the whole point of our Lord's love for His church, and thus the whole point of marriage. God truly hates divorce.

2 Remarriage for the innocent

In the previous chapter, we began examining the first of a few important New Testament texts on divorce and remarriage: Matthew 5:31–32 in Jesus' Sermon on the Mount. Now we get to the meat of what Jesus wanted to teach: 'I say to you that everyone who divorces his wife, except for the reason of unchastity, makes her commit adultery; and whoever marries a divorced woman commits adultery' (verse 32).

Here Jesus affirmed exactly what Moses was teaching in Deuteronomy 24: that unjustified divorce inevitably leads to adultery. To the legalistic, self-righteous scribes and Pharisees, He was essentially saying, 'You consider yourselves to be great teachers and keepers of the Law, but by allowing no-fault divorce, you have caused a great blight of adultery to contaminate God's people! By lowering God's standards to meet your own, you have led many people into sin and judgment.'

Confronted with a proper interpretation

The Pharisees interpreted Moses' instructions to mean, 'If you find something distasteful about your wife, go ahead and divorce her.' To them, doing the paperwork properly was the main issue. Jesus knew their interpretation was warped and thus confronted them with the text's true meaning.

One fundamental error in their thinking is boldly highlighted in Matthew 5:27–30. They comforted themselves with the notion that, as long as the legal forms were filled out properly, a divorce was perfectly lawful. *After all,* they reasoned, *divorce is preferable to adultery.*

But Jesus said, 'I say to you that everyone who looks at a woman with lust for her has already committed adultery with her in his heart' (verse 28). Then He showed them that no sacrifice is too great to maintain moral purity, making effective use of hyperbole to drive home His point:

If your right eye makes you stumble, tear it out and throw it from you; for it is better for you to lose one of the parts of your body, than for your whole body to be thrown into hell. If your right hand makes you stumble, cut it off and throw it from you; for it is better for you to lose one of the parts of your body, than for your whole body to go into hell (verses 29–30).

Then in verses 31–32 He pointed out that they had even given their approval to a system of institutionalized adultery by permitting easy divorce for almost any imaginable cause. He said that divorce and remarriage without a legitimate reason is itself tantamount to adultery. A little paperwork cannot legalize the evil lust that provokes men to abandon their wives and marry someone else. Far from being a means of *avoiding* adultery, the practice was itself tainted with all the same moral evils as the grossest act of fornication.

Moreover, Jesus indicated that in some ways divorce is even worse than adultery. That was made clear as He refuted the Pharisees' teaching with a proper interpretation of God's Law. He said that every time a man without proper cause turns his wife loose to remarry, he is responsible for causing her to commit an act of adultery, which makes him guilty also. In addition, the man who marries the former wife and the woman who marries the former husband are likewise guilty of adultery. So the result of divorce is *multiplied* adultery. Instead of avoiding adultery (as they thought), the Pharisees' liberal attitude toward divorce was actually breeding and proliferating adultery.

Our Lord was not adding to or modifying what Moses had said, but simply clarifying it. By divorcing his wife on grounds other than adultery, a husband makes the innocent former wife commit adultery if she remarries. That principle sets Moses' instructions about divorce in a much clearer light. Moses' law was portraying divorce as obviously something to be avoided rather than encouraged. Although the Old Testament law governing divorce was brief and left many questions unanswered, no one should ever have imagined that Moses' mere mention of divorce was meant to advocate the practice or make it easy to justify.

In fact, when Jesus taught in the Sermon on the Mount that divorce ought to be avoided if at all possible, He was by no means introducing a new concept. Although it wasn't stated explicitly in Deuteronomy 24:1–4 (the only place where Moses wrote about divorce), it was nevertheless a principle the Pharisees could have and should have gleaned from Malachi 2:16, where God says plainly that He hates divorce.

We, in turn, ought to glean an important lesson about biblical interpretation from the Pharisees' error: In order to understand the full meaning of Scripture, we must compare Scripture with Scripture, and allow the Bible to interpret itself.

Notice that Jesus *assumed* that a divorced woman would normally remarry. That was the whole idea behind divorce. It dissolved the marriage union in order to allow another marriage to take place. Jesus didn't envision divorce as a permanent legal separation, but as a provision in the civil law that makes way for a remarriage. So when He indicated that divorce is permissible in certain instances, He was also authorizing remarriage in those cases. Conversely, if a divorce takes place that is *not* permissible, remarriage in that case is tantamount to adultery.

Christ made the same point with slightly different words in Mark 10:11–13: 'Whoever divorces his wife and marries another woman commits adultery against her; and if she herself divorces her husband and marries another man, she is committing adultery.' Jesus' statement 'Whoever marries a divorced woman commits adultery' (Matthew 5:32; Luke 16:18) completes the picture: A man or woman who has no right to divorce has no right to remarry. To do so initiates a whole chain of adultery because remarriage after illegitimate divorce results in illegitimate and adulterous relationships for everyone concerned.

The detrimental effects of divorce

When we carefully consider the disastrous impact of divorce on children, other relatives, and society in general, it becomes obvious that few practices match divorce for sheer destructiveness. Divorce causes not only the multiplication of sin, but also confusion, resentment, hatred, bitterness, despair, conflict, and hardships of every sort.

Despite that, the Pharisees—like many people today—still had a hard time accepting Jesus' clear teaching on divorce and remarriage. Some time after the Sermon on the Mount, Jesus addressed this topic once again when He was tested by some Pharisees in Matthew 19. We will examine that interchange more carefully in future chapters, but for now, note how

Jesus summarized God's intention for marriage: "'For this reason a man shall leave his father and mother and be joined to his wife, and the two shall become one flesh" ... They are no longer two, but one flesh. What therefore God has joined together, let no man separate' (Matthew 19:5–6).

The Pharisees' response, 'Why then did Moses *command* to give her a certificate of divorce and send her away?' (emphasis added) again betrayed their misinterpretation of Deuteronomy 24:1–4. Jesus had to explain, 'Because of your hardness of heart, Moses *permitted* you to divorce your wives; but from the beginning it has not been this way' (verse 8, emphasis added). God never commanded divorce but only *permitted* it as a concession to sinful, self-willed mankind.

By the way, don't be confused by the fact that in Mark 10:5, Jesus Himself speaks of Deuteronomy 24:1–4 as a commandment. There He is referring to Moses' command *not to remarry* a person defiled by an illegitimate divorce. He is not suggesting that *divorce* is ever commanded anywhere in Scripture. It is not.

The exception clause

Jesus names only one condition where divorce is not the *cause* of adultery, and that is in cases where the marriage bond has already been destroyed by one party's infidelity. It is wrong to divorce one's spouse '*except for the reason of unchastity*' (Matthew 5:32, emphasis added).

Don't make the same kind of mistake the Pharisees made by thinking of this as a command. This one exception does not mean divorce is *necessary* when a spouse is unfaithful (as if God were eager for the divorce to take place). This is not a command, but a concession.

It is significant that sexual infidelity is the only legal basis Christ gave for divorce. He was highlighting the divine purpose for marriage 'from the beginning' (Matthew 19:8), and He stressed the fact that God's original design for marriage was one man and one woman entering into a permanent, indissoluble union with each other. Adultery—especially unrepentant or long-term unfaithfulness—constitutes a serious breach of that union, even apart from the formality of a divorce. Therefore, when Jesus named 'unchastity' as the sole grounds for divorce, He seemed to have in mind a worst-case scenario—a case in which divorce would simply be a legal acknowledgment that the permanent union had already been permanently and irreparably ruptured by the guilty person's sin.

(There is one additional case in which divorce is permissible, as stated by the Apostle Paul in 1 Corinthians 7:15, but before we consider that passage, we need to finish studying Jesus' teaching in Matthew 5 and 19. Jesus is laying the groundwork on which Paul—writing under the Holy Spirit's infallible guidance—later builds.)

People who wish to believe there are *no* biblical grounds at all for divorce point out that the exception clause appears only in Matthew's Gospel. They fear that taking it at face value would contradict or add to God's Law regarding the sin of adultery.

Of course, God has to say a thing only once for it to be true, so the fact that the exception clause appears only in Matthew has no bearing on its truthfulness. God doesn't say everything on a subject every time He brings it up. In Matthew 5 and 19 the clause is included specifically to correct the Pharisees' misrepresentation of God's Law regarding adultery. The exception clause in those passages amplifies Jesus' teaching on divorce in Mark 10 and Luke 16—it does not contradict it in any way.

Types of adultery

The one exception Jesus names ('except for the reason of unchastity'—Matthew 5:32) is easily misunderstood or misconstrued by some who try to give it too fine a meaning. (Some have suggested, for example, that it applies only to infidelity during the betrothal period, because if Jesus wanted to signify post-marital adultery, He would have used a more specific word.) But actually, the word 'unchastity' is deliberately broad rather than specific.

In the Greek text, Jesus employs the word *porneia*, which is capable of a broad range of meanings. It is a general term for fornication (illicit sexual intercourse), but it can also apply to various kinds of lascivious or immoral behavior, ranging from a moral flaw in one's character (such as an obsessive addiction to pornography) to the act of bestiality—or even worse. It's not the specific Greek word for adultery, which would be *moicheia*—but certainly *includes* adultery. Both the context and the spirit of Jesus' remarks suggest that He has in mind serious sins involving deliberate infidelity, and He says nothing to indicate that what he is describing is limited to sins that take place during betrothal.

Because Matthew 5:31–32 focuses on marriage and divorce, it would seem obvious that the primary unchastity Jesus had in mind here was in fact adultery. But *porneia* was also broad enough to include sins like incest (fornication involving blood relatives, legal relatives, or children), prostitution, homosexuality, and bestiality. Those were the same sexual acts for which the Old Testament demanded the death penalty (Leviticus 20:10–16; Deuteronomy 22:21). Any of those—or the deliberate practice of any similar perverted sexual activities—would therefore be grounds for divorce.

Jesus and Moses stand together

Notice that Jesus gave no more approval for divorce than Moses did. God's Old Testament ideal has not been changed. The permissions for divorce in Moses' day were designed to meet the unique, practical problems of an imperfect, sinful people.

God never *condoned* divorce because He does not want that which He has joined together to be rent asunder—and 'woe to the one who quarrels with his Maker!' (Isaiah 45:9). That's exactly why adultery (another sinful reality that God never intended)—specifically the hard-hearted adultery of an inveterately unfaithful spouse—is the only thing that makes divorce permissible. When the bond of marriage has already been irreparably broken by such a sin, then—and only then—is divorce an option.

As a matter of fact, under the strictest application of the Old Testament Law, adultery would lead to the permanent and irreversible dissolution of the marriage because the guilty party was put to death (Leviticus 20:10).

Why was divorce an option for adultery, rather than death by stoning?

The change from death to divorce for adultery

It will help us to have a right understanding of Jesus' teaching on divorce if we see that Jesus and Moses are in perfect agreement on this issue. Remember: Jesus was not overturning or modifying Moses' law in any way. He specifically said that He did not come to contradict or annul the least part of the Law (Matthew 5:18–19). So when He then mentioned sexual infidelity as the one reason that can make divorce permissible

(Matthew 5:32; 19:9), He was implicitly acknowledging the great latitude for showing mercy that was built into the Old Testament penal system. As a matter of fact, Scripture does clearly imply that even under Moses' law, divorce could take the place of execution by stoning as an alternative, more merciful, penalty for someone caught in adultery. Joseph, for instance, 'a righteous man,' was prepared at first to divorce Mary rather than stone her for her presumed adultery (Matthew 1:19).

So why did God sometimes allow divorce instead of always demanding the death penalty? Part of the answer may be that Israel had so completely immersed itself in immorality that there was not sufficient desire for righteousness left in the people to carry out executions for that offense. More importantly, it seems clear that God Himself mercifully chose not to enforce the death penalty strictly and rigidly in every case. We see a glimpse of that in the compassion of Jesus, who successfully challenged Pharisees who were about to stone a woman caught in the act of adultery, and then forgave her Himself (John 8:3–11).

That the death penalty was prescribed for adultery shows what a serious sin marital infidelity is in God's eyes. Remember that rebellious children could also be punished with death by stoning under Moses' law (Deuteronomy 21:18–21). That likewise shows what God thinks of adolescent rebellion. Although those were the maximum penalties allowable under the Law, there is no record that such penalties were ever used on a widespread basis in Israel. They seem to have been reserved for rare and very extreme cases of gross and incorrigible sin.

Apparently, rather than always demanding that the death penalty be carried out, the aggrieved spouse could opt for divorce. Once again, divorce was never regarded as a *good* option, but it was usually deemed a better and more merciful option than death by stoning. That, in a thumbnail, is what Jesus meant when He said that divorce was permitted by God only because of the hardness of the human heart (Matthew 19:8). In Chapter 4, we will study in greater detail what Jesus meant when He spoke of the hardness of the human heart.

But bear in mind for now that divorce was never *commanded*, even for adultery. Otherwise God would have ordered Hosea to divorce Gomer. Just as divorce was better than stoning because it was more merciful, likewise forgiveness and reconciliation, when possible, are better than divorce. So a legitimate bill of divorce was *allowable* for adultery, but it was never commanded or required.

There are times, sadly, when the sinning partner refuses to repent or be restored. Those are the times when divorce becomes an option—always only as a last resort, when the unrepentant adulterer finally exhausts the patience of the innocent spouse.

Protection for the innocent

Whenever an adulterer was put to death under the *strictest* application of Moses' law, the innocent partner would, of course, be free to remarry. As we have noted, real-life instances where the death sentence was actually executed against adulterers seem to have been fairly rare. (David, for example, wasn't condemned to death for his adultery with Bathsheba.)

Moses' provision for divorce (rather than death by stoning) was actually a compassionate alternative to death by stoning. It was permitted for mercy's sake—first, showing mercy to the *guilty* spouse by sparing his or her life; and second, showing mercy to the *innocent* spouse by clearing the way for remarriage. To permit the divorce but deny remarriage would actually turn mercy on its head by sentencing the innocent party to a life of loneliness and misery.

As a matter of fact, divorce formally and legally dissolved the marriage for this very purpose: so that the aggrieved partner would be free to remarry without any guilt or stigma.

That is precisely what Jesus is teaching here, and it is the only reasonable interpretation of the exception clause: Adultery (or the equivalent)— especially when it becomes a persistent pattern—may be legitimate grounds for divorce. And in such cases, the innocent spouse is free to remarry after divorce.

What about the hard questions Jesus didn't answer?

Jesus, like Moses before Him, didn't give explicit answers to all the questions His teaching on divorce might raise in real life. For example, after a divorce is final and the innocent spouse remarries, if the guilty party then truly repents and forsakes his or her adulterous ways, is that person then free to remarry also?

Scripture nowhere deals with that question or dozens like it.

Unfortunately, divorce usually creates a tangled mess of broken lives and broken relationships. To set the aftermath of every divorce right again would be a task comparable to unscrambling an omelet made of a billion eggs. Some of the practical dilemmas that are created by divorce simply have no clear biblical solutions. Biblical counselors, and repentant Christians seeking to honor God by sorting out the ramifications of their past sins, sometimes simply have to do the best they can with the principles Scripture does give.

One such principle is the glorious reality that when a sinner comes to faith in Christ for the first time, he or she becomes (in effect) a new creature with a whole new life principle and a new, purified heart. 'Therefore if anyone is in Christ, he is a new creature; the old things passed away; behold, new things have come' (2 Corinthians 5:17). Just as Mary Magdalene's past guilt and shame were totally erased and became utterly irrelevant when Christ saved her (Luke 8:2), likewise every genuine believer's pre-conversion sins say nothing about the person's true character now, and therefore should not ordinarily be a factor in determining whether the person is fit for ministry, remarriage, or leadership in the church. We should leave those sins and their memory (as much as possible) where they belong—in the past.

Obviously, some sins *do* have consequences that pursue the sinner from his or her past life. Civil crimes, for example, involve penalties that must be paid to society. Convicted criminals don't (and shouldn't) get out of prison automatically when they become believers in Christ. The penalty to society still needs to be paid. Likewise, those who have wronged others should be like Zaccheus, who made restitution to his many victims when he forsook his life of sin and became a believer (Luke 19:8).

But when we are saved, the moral guilt and the spiritual stigma of our past sins are done away forever because of the work of Christ on our behalf. If a person has paid his or her debt to society and furnished proof of a truly transformed life, there is normally no reason why his or her past life should be cited as a reason to forbid remarriage or disqualify the person from ministry. The Apostle Paul's past sins—grievous though they were—did not disqualify him from apostleship (1 Timothy 1:12–13).

When a person sins as an unbeliever and those sins are responsible for the destruction of a marriage, if that person later becomes a Christian, he or she should first do everything possible to make restitution and seek forgiveness from all who were wronged by the sin, starting with the aggrieved spouse. If both partners are still unmarried and both are now believers, it might well be possible to restore the marriage. In such a case, the person *should* seek reconciliation and restoration of the marriage as part of the duty of making restitution. But where restoration of the marriage is impossible; or in cases where remarriage would involve an unequal yoke with an unbeliever; or if there is some other factor that would compound the sin that caused the divorce in the first place—as long as all the sins that led to the dissolution of the marriage have been abandoned and forgiven, I see no reason to forbid the repentant person from remarrying.

But what if the guilty party was already a professing believer when the sin that caused the divorce occurred? In that case, the situation is somewhat more complex. Notice that in 1 Timothy 1:13, the Apostle Paul says his past blasphemy and persecution of the church did not disqualify him from apostleship *because he committed those sins in ignorance and unbelief.* Had he committed those or similar sins as a believer, he would indeed have been disqualified from church leadership because his testimony as a Christian would not have been above reproach (1 Timothy 3:2; Titus 1:6).

That is not to suggest that the sins we commit as Christians are somehow worse or harder to forgive than the sins we commit as unbelievers. The sins we commit as believers are covered by the blood of Christ just as surely as the sins we committed before.

But the stigma is not so easily erased. The deliberate sin of a Christian reflects a character flaw that undermines the person's testimony and trustworthiness. As a pastor, I would not consent to remarry a person who was unfaithful to a previous spouse while professing faith in Christ. If that person's original profession of faith meant so little, how is it possible to know whether a subsequent profession of repentance is legitimate?

At the same time, I'm not prepared to state dogmatically that such a person can never, under any circumstances, remarry. Since Scripture is silent on the matter, I wouldn't want to place limits on the grace and mercy of God where He himself does not explicitly draw such boundaries.

So here is my best counsel to the person in such a situation: *Scrutinize your heart carefully, and examine your life thoroughly for the fruits of authentic repentance. Don't consider remarriage at all unless you have proved yourself faithful over a period of time equal to or greater than the duration of the sin. True faithfulness would include your involvement in a sound church. Seek the counsel of your pastor and qualified elders, and submit to their judgment.*

Until repentance is truly complete and all those factors have been considered—with the result that all involved would agree that the person's life has been fundamentally set in order—remarriage is utterly out of the question. In such cases, Paul's words in 1 Corinthians 7:10–11 would seem to provide the best biblical counsel, and it applies to men as well as women, when they are separated from their spouses without legitimate grounds: 'A wife is not to depart from her husband. But even if she does depart, *let her remain unmarried*' (New King James Version, emphasis added).

In the best of circumstances, of course, where churches routinely follow the instructions of Matthew 18:15–20, many instances of marital infidelity can be arrested and dealt with before the situation ends in divorce. In cases where a person persists in hard-hearted or unrepentant adultery and a divorce ultimately results, the guilty party should be pursued through the process outlined in Matthew 18. If that person nevertheless refuses all appeals for repentance, in the end he or she is to be regarded as an unbeliever (Matthew 18:17). Perhaps that is why Scripture never expressly deals with the question of what to do about a Christian whose adultery causes a divorce and who later repents. Most such people are very likely unbelievers to begin with, and their subsequent repentance (if truly genuine) actually represents an initial act of saving faith.

By my reading of Scripture, that is how divorce between a couple in the church would almost certainly have been regarded in apostolic times. The guilty party would have been put out of the church and regarded as an unbeliever. If he or she did subsequently repent, that act of repentance would most likely have been understood by all (including that person) as a first-time response of true saving faith. It would, after all, reflect the abandonment of the most hard-hearted variety of unbelief.

That question (and many others like it) is confusing in our day only because of contemporary evangelicalism's tendency to diminish the quality of authentic faith. One thing that is neither confusing nor ambiguous is the overriding truth of Jesus' teaching about divorce: God *still* hates divorce. In Matthew 19, which we begin studying in earnest in the next chapter, Jesus set the record straight about that. God's ideal continues to be monogamous, lifelong marriage.

Why divorce was never God's intention

Some years ago, a journalist for a national news magazine asked rhetorically, 'Are there any persons left in the land who have not heard a friend or a child or a parent describe the agony of divorce?' Divorce has become pandemic, to the point that hardly a person can be found who has not been affected by it either directly or indirectly. Many marriages seem to be little more than a socially recognized battleground where warfare between the spouses is the rule and harmony the exception.

Mind-numbing statistics

Each year around the world, there are millions of divorces, and beneath the rubble of mind-numbing statistics lie the crushed lives of men, women, and children. None of them escapes suffering and damage, no matter how amicable the divorce may be. Nearly every state in America has enacted 'no fault' divorce laws, making divorce almost as easy as marriage. It is not surprising, therefore, that the largest caseloads in civil courts today relate to family disputes.

Past reasons for family stability

In past years, the vast majority of marriages held together, and divorce was difficult and rare. The reasons for that stability are not hard to find. First was the moral force of the family. Not only the immediate family but also the extended family of grandparents, aunts and uncles, and cousins was the center of personal loyalty and activity. That extended family was usually bound together by a shared tradition of moral and religious convictions. All the family members—adults as well as children—knew they could depend on those loved ones for help, comfort, encouragement, and security. But as moral permissiveness, feminism, skepticism, humanism, easier mobility, and the disruptive and worldly influences of television, movies, and other media began to undermine the family unit, divorce rapidly increased. The numbers of young mothers working outside the home and single adults living apart from any close family relationship have also increased dramatically, adding to the decrease of family support, encouragement, and influence.

The second reason for family stability in the past was community expectation. Society in general and the legal system in particular recognized, strongly supported, and protected the primacy of the family as well as a biblically based morality. Strict laws made divorce difficult, and community ethics and peer pressure made the stigma of it severe. In great contrast, the subject of divorce is treated very lightly now. I remember thinking my California, USA culture had hit a new low when I saw a newspaper ad that said: 'Divorce $25 ... Unload That Turkey!' Something my grandmother used to say came to mind: 'Perish the thought!' Husbands and wives, like all people, are made in the image of God. Divorce is rightly viewed as a blight and a dread. The sacred bond of marriage is being ruptured at a fearsome rate, but few in the community seem to care anymore.

The third and strongest of forces that helped maintain family stability was the teaching of the church. Until modern times, every branch of Christendom—Catholic, Orthodox, and Protestant—strongly supported family life and just as strongly opposed divorce. But as their constituencies pled for concessions to worldly standards and practices, church bodies acquiesced. Families have suffered the bitter consequences of those compromises ever since. Churches that mimic the world's perspective will seek to emasculate biblical doctrine. God will not stand by silently, 'For it is time for judgment to begin with the household of God; and if it begins with us first, what will be the outcome for those who do not obey the gospel of God?' (1 Peter 4:17).

Ignored or twisted but never better

In the name of Christian love, some individuals and groups not only condone divorce, but even insist that it is sometimes God's will. A well-known entertainer claimed that her divorce was justified because her husband was a detriment to her career. She claimed that she did not believe her divorce related to her religious beliefs in any significant way and that, even if the divorce really was wrong, God loved her in spite of it—as if divorce made no real difference to God. Unless that poor woman sincerely repents, how will she face the God who said, 'I hate divorce … So take heed to your spirit, that you do not deal treacherously' (Malachi 2:16)?

I received the following letter from a lady in our church:

> My husband walked out in February and called two weeks later to tell me he wanted a divorce. He said that God had given him a perfect peace about it, so it was surely God's will. He tried to convince me God allowed divorce because the feeling of love was gone and thereby we were no longer compatible. Our former pastor told him that if he wasn't in love with me and saw no hope for our marriage, he ought to get a divorce. A 'Christian' marriage counselor told him the very same thing.

That isn't what the Bible teaches; that's what the scribes and Pharisees believed.

Even when Christians go to Scripture for guidance concerning divorce and remarriage, they often do so with preconceptions and predispositions that make responsible interpretation elusive. Some people consult the Bible solely to find justification for views they already hold. Others fall into the trap either of adding to or taking away from what it teaches. To justify divorce and hopefully ease people's feelings, some people lower the biblical standard in the name of love. To try to stem the tide of divorce and promote spirituality, others raise the standard higher than the Bible teaches. But that which is contrary to Scripture can never be loving or spiritual. A human standard may be more lenient or more restrictive than Scripture, but it can never be better. When God's Word is ignored or perverted in any area, tragedy is always the consequence. That is especially true regarding marriage and the intertwined lives involved.

Jesus on the hot seat

Matthew 19:1–12 gives a clear discourse on God's revelation about marriage and divorce. It came when Jesus left Galilee 'and came into the region of Judea beyond the Jordan [River]' (verse 1). This was in the days when He was determined to go to Jerusalem for the Passover, knowing His time was drawing near to be offered as the Lamb of God who takes away the sin of the world. 'Large crowds followed Him, and He healed them there' (verse 2), thus demonstrating His compassion and messianic credentials. Into this tender and wondrous scene 'some Pharisees came to Jesus, testing Him, and asking, "Is it lawful for a man to divorce his wife for any reason at all?"' (verse 3).

Almost from the beginning of His ministry, Jesus had been criticized by the Pharisees, who even before this time had become His arch-enemies and planned to kill Him (Matthew 12:14). They were the largest and most influential party in the Jewish religious establishment of that day. Their unbiblical traditions and hypocritical lifestyles were the antithesis of true righteousness, said Jesus in His Sermon on the Mount (Matthew 5:20). They despised Jesus because He undermined their false teaching and exposed their deceitful living.

Therefore, when they came to Him now, they wanted to discredit Him in the eyes of the people so that He would lose His popularity and be easier for them to destroy. Their test question was well thought out, carefully calculated to place Him at odds with Moses, the great giver of God's Law.

Chauvinistic extremes

For many centuries, divorce had been a volatile issue for debate among the Jewish people. In the battle of the sexes since Genesis 3, of the women's liberation and male chauvinism that have resulted, male chauvinism has been the dominant of those two perversions throughout history because men are naturally stronger. In many cultures even today, women are treated more like animals than human beings, and wives treated more like possessions to be bought and traded than partners to be loved and cherished. The Pharisees, because of their spurious, self-serving interpretations of the Mosaic Law to justify their lusts for other women, had become the leading promoters of easy divorce.

At the other extreme was an opposing and much less influential faction of rabbis, represented by Rabbi Shammai, a near contemporary of Jesus, who maintained that divorce was never permissible. That narrow-minded, hard-line view was not only unpopular but, like the liberal position of the Pharisees, was also unscriptural.

Representing the liberal Pharisaic view was Rabbi Hillel, who also lived about that time. He taught that a man could divorce his wife for the most trivial reasons, for such things as taking her hair down in public, talking to other men, burning the bread, or putting too much salt in the food. For her to speak ill of her mother-in-law, be infertile, or not give birth to a son was more than sufficient grounds for divorce among this popular set. This viewpoint is just another version of the wicked 'Unload That Turkey!' mentality. It appeals to mankind at the lowest level.

A clever trap

From His previous teaching, the Pharisees knew that Jesus did not hold to such a liberalized view of divorce. Remember, they had heard Him say that 'Everyone who divorces his wife, except for the reason of unchastity, makes her commit adultery; and whoever marries a divorced woman commits adultery' (Matthew 5:32). They now expected Him to take the same stand and thereby alienate and intimidate the many other Jewish people besides themselves who accepted the idea of divorce for any cause at all. They hoped to discredit Him by identifying Him in the minds of the people with the narrow and intolerant view of the Shammai school of thought. Similar tactics occur today, especially in the political arena. The Pharisees were the original spin doctors.

Ultimately, of course, they wanted to destroy our Lord. The clever Pharisees were well aware that the part of Judea where Jesus was currently ministering was under the jurisdiction of Herod Antipas. He was the Herod who had John the Baptist imprisoned and eventually beheaded for condemning his unlawful marriage to Herodias, whom he had seduced away from his brother Philip (Matthew 14:3–12). No doubt the Pharisees hoped that, by denouncing divorce for any cause at all, Jesus would thereby publicly condemn Herod's adulterous relationship just as John had done—and suffer John's fate.

A stinging rebuke

Yes, that was a very clever, sinister trap, but the Pharisees had no idea of whom they were up against. Jesus indeed 'knew all men, and … did not need anyone to testify concerning man, for He Himself knew what was in man' (John 2:24–25). Piercing into the depths of their dark hearts, Jesus answered,

Have you not read that He who created them from the beginning made them male and female, and said, 'For this reason a man shall leave his father and mother and be joined to his wife, and the two shall become one flesh'? So they are no longer two, but one flesh. What therefore God has joined together, let no man separate (Matthew 19:4–6).

Instead of giving a direct yes or no to the Pharisees' question about divorce in verse 3, Jesus went beyond rabbinical tradition, and even further back than the laws of Moses. He went all the way back to God's creation of Adam and Eve.

Jesus' opening words had nothing directly to do with the question of divorce but were a stinging rebuke to the learned Pharisees, who prided themselves on their great knowledge of Scripture. Responding to their question with a question of His own, Jesus was in effect saying, 'Have you not read even the Book of Genesis? Don't you know the very first thing God said about marriage? Don't you recall that He who created them from the beginning made them male and female, and said, "For this reason a man shall leave his father and mother, and be joined to his wife, and the two shall become one flesh"?' By quoting from Genesis 1:27 and 2:24, Jesus was saying, 'Your argument is not with Me, but with God.' Jesus was not being evasive, as many people today are when questioned by the media, but got straight to the heart of the matter.

Four reasons why divorce was never God's intention

From those two verses, taken from the first two chapters of Scripture, the Lord presented four reasons why divorce was never God's intention. First, He said that God 'created them from the beginning … male and female' (Matthew 19:4). In the Hebrew text of Genesis 1:27, 'male and female' are in the emphatic position, giving the sense of *the* one male and *the* one female. God did not create a group of males and females who could pick and choose mates as it suited them. There were no spares or options—no Adam, Eve, and Steve! There was no provision, or even possibility, for multiple or alternate spouses. Only one man and one woman existed in the beginning. For that very obvious reason, divorce and remarriage were not options in the divine plan for man.

A principle to be projected and applied

Second, Jesus said, 'For this reason a man shall leave his father and mother and be joined to his wife' (Matthew 19:5). Since Adam and Eve had no parents to leave, the leaving of father and mother was a principle to be projected into and applied to all future generations. The Hebrew word behind 'joined to' refers to a strong bonding together or being stuck together—but a happy stuck, not a sad stuck! Marriage binds two hearts, diligently and utterly committed to pursuing each other in love, stuck together in an indissoluble bond, glued in mind, will, spirit, and emotion. The psalmist used the same Hebrew word to describe how his heart was glued to God's Word, saying, 'I cling to Your testimonies; O LORD' (Psalm 119:31). Job used that word when he spoke of his bones clinging to his skin (Job 19:20). It is used to speak of Ruth clinging to her mother-in-law, Naomi (Ruth 1:14) and of the men of Judah remaining steadfastly loyal to King David (2 Samuel 20:2).

Consecration and commitment

This idea of a close bonding and deep interpersonal relationship is seen in the modern Hebrew word for marriage, *kiddushin*, which is closely related to the terms for 'holy' and 'sanctified'. Marriage, as God has always intended it to be, involves the total commitment and consecration of husbands and wives to each other, and to Him as the divine author of their union and witness to their covenant. Its highest purpose is as a picture or symbol of the believer's everlasting union with Christ. Paul wrote to the Corinthian church, 'I am jealous for you with a godly jealousy; for I betrothed you to one husband, so that to Christ I might present you as a pure virgin' (2 Corinthians 11:2). We see that marriage to our Creator ultimately taking place at the end of the ages in the Book of Revelation, where Christ is pictured as the bridegroom and His people as the bride (Revelation 19:7–9; 21:1–3). The Bible, from beginning to end—from Genesis to Revelation—affirms that marriage is sacred and lofty. Therefore, 'Marriage is to be held in honor among all; and the marriage bed is to be undefiled; for fornicators and adulterers God will judge' (Hebrews 13:4). The greatest honor of marriage is that it proclaims to the world as a symbol the union between Christ and His own blessed church.

Our marriages are to be as permanent, satisfying, as full of love, and as absolutely binding as Christ's relationship is to His church.

The one-flesh aspect of marriage

The third reason Jesus gave for divorce not being God's intention is that, in marriage, the two become one flesh. As the Apostle Paul declares in 1 Corinthians 7:4, husbands and wives belong to each other in the physical relationship of marriage: 'The wife does not have authority over her own body, but the husband does; and likewise also the husband does not have authority over his own body, but the wife does.'

When a man and woman are joined in marriage, 'they are no longer two, but one flesh,' said the Lord (Matthew 19:6). They are therefore indivisible and inseparable, except through death. In God's eyes, the two become one. They become the total possession of each other; one in mind and spirit, in goals and direction, in emotion and will. When they have a child, that child becomes the perfect demonstration of their oneness since he or she is a unique reflection of the fusion of two people into one flesh, and carries the combined traits of both parents.

Some people foolishly argue, however, that the sexual act of becoming one flesh is what essentially constitutes a marriage. If that were true, there would be no such thing as fornication because as soon as an unmarried man and woman became one flesh, they would automatically be married rather than guilty of wickedness. Under the Mosaic Law, the act of fornication obligated the man to marry the woman or pay compensation to her father (Exodus 22:16–17), further indicating that the sexual act itself is not the equivalent of marriage.

On the other hand, the act of adultery—shattering as it is to the marriage relationship—does not in itself dissolve a marriage. Marriage is a mutual covenant, a God-ordained obligation between a man and a woman to lifelong companionship. Recall from Malachi 2:14 that God rebuked the treachery of the Israelite men for divorcing their wives, describing each wife as 'your companion and your wife by covenant.' In God's eyes, every wife is a 'wife by covenant,' never merely a wife by fornication, convenience, or whim.

Every marriage made in heaven

The fourth reason Jesus gave for divorce not being in God's perfect design is that, in the creative sense, every marriage is made in heaven. From the very first marriage, that of Adam and Eve, God has joined together every husband and wife. Marriage is first of all God's institution and God's doing, regardless of how men may corrupt it and deny or disregard His part in it. Whether it is between Christians or between atheists or idolaters, whether it is arranged by the parents or by the mutual desire and consent of the bride and bridegroom, marriage is above all the handiwork of God for the procreation, pleasure, and preservation of the human race. Whether it is entered into wisely or foolishly, sincerely or insincerely, selfishly or unselfishly, with great or little commitment, God's design for every marriage is that it be permanent until the death of one of the spouses.

God engineered man and woman to complement, support, and give joy to each other through the mutual commitment of the marriage bond. It is by His divine hand that they are created to fulfill each other, encourage each other, strengthen each other, and produce children as fruit of their love for each other. Whether they recognize it or not, every couple who has enjoyed the companionship, happiness, and fulfillment of marriage has experienced the wondrous blessing of God. The Apostle Peter, therefore, described marriage as 'the grace of life' (1 Peter 3:7), which is like saying it is the whipped cream on top! There is no good thing in marriage that is not derived from God Himself.

What divorce and abortion have in common

No child can be conceived by the procreative act of a man and woman who is not first conceived by the creative act of God. Psalm 139:16, looking at life from the perspective of the child in the womb, says, 'Your eyes have seen my unformed substance; and in Your book were all written the days that were ordained for me, when as yet there was not one of them.' Every marriage and every child is a creation of God. Divorce and abortion, therefore, share this evil common denominator: They kill a creation of God.

To destroy a marriage is to destroy a creation of Almighty God. 'What therefore God has joined together,' Jesus warned, 'let no man separate'

(Matthew 19:6). In the context of marriage, the Greek word translated 'separate' (*chorizo*) always carries the meaning of divorce, not a mere separation. It is translated 'leave' in 1 Corinthians 7:10, which, as we soon will see, unequivocally speaks of divorce in the English text as well as the Greek. Jesus' point is that marriage is always the work of God, whereas divorce is always the work of man. No man—whoever he is or for whatever reason he may have—has the right to separate what God has joined together.

4 Divorce and the hardness of the human heart

In Matthew 19 we are learning that Jesus let us see into the very heart of God on the subject of marriage as He established it from the beginning. His arch-opponents used that subject to bait Him into a carefully contrived trap. They hopelessly underestimated Him, however, so as we left them in the last chapter, they were the ones looking trapped like rats. How did they respond? Was it, 'Oh yes, now we see! Thank you for getting us back in line with God's truth, for truly "man does not live by bread alone, but ... by everything that proceeds out of the mouth of the LORD"' (Deuteronomy 8:3)? No, their minds were already made up to do what they wanted to do, and they were not willing to be dissuaded by the facts of God's Word. They did not want to appear that way to others, however.

Not interested

No doubt anticipating Jesus' appeal to Scripture, the Pharisees were prepared with what they considered to be a scriptural rebuttal. They replied to Jesus, 'Why then did Moses command to give her a certificate of divorce and send her away?' (Matthew 19:7). They were so intent on defending their own fleshly standards and on trying to discredit and destroy Jesus that they totally disregarded what He had just said. They were not interested in the divine standard for marriage that God had established at creation, but were bent on defending their own low, self-centered standards. They are classic examples of people looking for moral and spiritual loopholes to accommodate their vices. On the one hand, these types want to be thought of as keeping God's Law because that is how they think they earn God's favor. On the other hand, they want to find every way out they possibly can, so exceptions are what interest them. These kinds of people don't really care about what God truly wants. What could be worse than to be one of them? What could be better than to cease being one of them?

Feigning divine support

To give the appearance of divine support for their liberal divorce customs, the Pharisees appealed to Moses, seeking to pit Jesus against God's great lawgiver. Because it is the only passage in the five books of Moses that mentions any grounds for divorce (legitimate or illegitimate), the passage the Pharisees referred to had to be Deuteronomy 24:1–4. As we saw in Chapter 1 while studying Matthew 5:31, the Deuteronomy passage clearly does not command divorce, as the Pharisees claimed. It mentions the giving of a certificate of divorce, without commenting on the propriety of that procedure. The only command in the passage relates to the issue of remarriage, not to divorce. Because the penalty for adultery was death in Moses' era, whatever indecency over which the man in Deuteronomy 24 divorced his wife must have come short of adultery. Vile as it might have been, it was obviously not sufficient grounds for divorce since the wife became defiled by adultery when remarrying. In God's eyes, she was still the wife of the first husband. That is why John the Baptist declared that Herod and Herodias were living in adultery despite the fact that a fancy marriage had taken place. In God's sight, Herodias was not Herod's wife but still 'the wife of his brother Philip' (Matthew 14:3).

God's reluctant permission

How did Jesus respond to the Pharisees' wrong interpretation? He said to them, 'Because of your hardness of heart Moses permitted you to divorce your wives; but from the beginning it has not been this way. And I say to you, whoever divorces his wife, except for immorality, and marries another woman commits adultery' (Matthew 19:8–9). After clarifying that God's Law did not commend, much less command, divorce, Jesus affirmed that it did permit divorce under one condition. Speaking to them as personal representatives of their fleshly forefathers, Jesus told the Pharisees that it was only because of the hardness of their hearts that Moses permitted them to divorce their wives.

However, in no Old Testament passage, including Deuteronomy 24:1–4, is specific permission for divorce given. One reason is not hard to surmise:

Since the Israelites so abused implied permission for divorce, how much more would they have abused explicit permission?

Because of His loving grace, God did not always exact the death penalty for adultery under the Mosaic covenant. Israel's later history gives instances of adultery that did not lead to execution. King David was strongly rebuked and severely punished for his adultery with Bathsheba, but he was not put to death. When the prophet Nathan confronted David and David humbly confessed, saying, 'I have sinned against the LORD,' Nathan replied, 'The LORD also has taken away your sin; you shall not die' (2 Samuel 12:13). David's successor, King Solomon, because of his hundreds of wives and concubines, lived in virtual unremitting adultery on the basis of the one-man, one-woman standard of Genesis 1–2. Yet, like his father, he did not suffer the death penalty.

The kings and people of Israel kept getting worse and worse, however, thinking lightly of the riches of God's kindness and tolerance and patience, not knowing that the kindness of God was intended to bring them to repentance. Because of their 'stubbornness and unrepentant heart,' they stored up wrath for themselves (Romans 2:4–5), and it ultimately broke out like floodwaters in the form of the Babylonian army.

Divorce following the violation of intermarriage with idolaters

When Jewish exiles returned from seventy years of captivity in Babylon, they sought to restore the Temple in Jerusalem and begin living according to God's Word. A major crisis they faced was over their intermarriages with pagan women, which were a violation of Deuteronomy 7:3–4: 'You shall not intermarry with them; you shall not give your daughters to their sons, nor shall you take their daughters for your sons. For they will turn your sons away from following Me to serve other gods; then the anger of the LORD will be kindled against you.' The Israelites decided to put away their pagan wives and the children born of those marriages. They came to that decision under the leadership of Ezra, 'a scribe skilled in the law of Moses' who 'set his heart to study the law of the LORD and to practice it, and to teach His statues and ordinances in Israel' (Ezra 7:6, 10; 10:1–44). Ezra was a godly man the people could trust as a spiritual leader and teacher.

Although there is no record that this divorce action was specifically approved by God, the lack of any condemnation implies that the resulting divorces were permitted by Him. Ezra himself said to his people, 'Make confession to the LORD God of your fathers and do His will; and separate yourselves from the ... foreign wives' (Ezra 10:11). Ezra wanted them to obey God's clearly revealed will in Deuteronomy 7 that forbade intermarriage with idolaters. Divorce is evil, so the situation in Ezra was a matter of choosing the lesser of two evils. The human heart is hard. It 'is more deceitful than all else and is desperately sick; who can understand it?' (Jeremiah 17:9). God does.

The historical context of Ezra supports the idea that those divorces were permitted by God on the grounds of adultery. Not only were all pagans of that day idolatrous, which Scripture repeatedly refers to as spiritual adultery, but also their regular rites and ceremonies involved gross immorality. It is therefore likely that the foreign wives the Israelite men had married were both physical and spiritual adulterers, thereby giving their husbands legitimate grounds for divorce.

God's own marriage and divorce

In a display of divine love and condescension second only to the Lord Jesus Christ's 'taking the form of a bond-servant, and being made in the likeness of men' (Philippians 2:7), God married Israel. But like Hosea's wife, Gomer, Israel was unfaithful. God therefore rebuked His bride Israel for her spiritual adultery in worshiping pagan deities. Treating the Israelites for the moment like children, He asked, 'Where is the certificate of divorce by which I have sent your mother away?' (Isaiah 50:1). The answer was that God had not given such a certificate because, just as Hosea with Gomer, God was not ready to divorce Israel, despite her constant adulteries committed against Him. Israel had no freedom from her relationship to God that would allow her to consummate relations with other so-called gods.

Finally, however, after pleading with His people for hundreds of years to forsake idolatry and return to Him, God did something startling. 'Have you seen what faithless Israel did?' He asked the prophet Jeremiah. 'She went up on every high hill and under every green tree, and she was a harlot there. I thought, "After she has done all these things, she will return to Me"; but she did not return.' Because of Israel's *unrelenting hardness of heart* in persisting with her unfaithfulness, God made a decision: 'I had sent her away and given her a writ of divorce' (Jeremiah 3:6–8). It was on the basis of her unrepentant and incessant spiritual adultery that God, so to speak, finally gave Israel a certificate of divorce.

That does not mean, however, that you and I are free to divorce our spouses for spiritual adultery, for something they do in their minds. Divorce as a legitimate action against adultery, as it filters down to human beings, is permitted only for the physical act of unrepentant adultery. Keep in mind also that God showed hundreds of years of patience toward adulterous Israel. That is a far cry from: 'My husband committed adultery [once], so that is the end of our marriage!' On the other hand, it is wrong for anyone, whatever his or her motive, to say there are no biblical grounds for divorce. By God's own example, divorce is approved in a prolonged, unrepentant, irreconcilable case of adultery.

Hope for the future

The case of Israel is a hopeful example of spiritual life after divorce. It even opens up the possibility of restoration in extraordinary cases where the divorced partners have not yet remarried. Although for many generations the Old Testament Israelites had committed serial acts of spiritual adultery through repeated dalliances with pagan religions (resulting in the writ of divorce described in Jeremiah 3:6–8), after returning from the Babylonian Exile, national Israel generally abstained from the frivolous pursuit of heathen gods. In other words, while the Israelites were spiritually unfaithful to Jehovah, they never 'married' themselves to the false gods with which they flirted (just as Gomer had never married any of her lovers). Because of His matchless grace, God declared that in a time yet future He would take Israel back to Himself:

'Behold, days are coming,' declares the LORD, 'when I will make a new covenant with the house of Israel and with the house of Judah, not like the covenant which I made with their fathers in the day I took them by the hand to bring them out of the land of Egypt, My covenant which they broke, although I was a husband to them,' declares the LORD. 'But this is the covenant which I will make with the house of Israel after those days,' declares the LORD, 'I will put My law within them and on their heart I will write it; and I will be their God, and they shall be My people' (Jeremiah 31:31–33).

In light of God's spiritual divorce and eventual remarriage to Israel, it is not right to claim that Scripture recognizes no grounds at all for divorce and remarriage, as some ancient rabbis claimed and as some Christians still claim today. God does not give us illustrations of His own righteous behavior that we cannot follow or apply. Since He finally divorced adulterous and unrepentant Israel after long years of forgiveness and mercy, it cannot be wrong for a man or woman to divorce an adulterous and unrepentant partner under similar circumstances. Since God makes it clear, however, that He hates divorce and permits it only because of the hardness of the human heart, divorce should never be pursued hastily or offhandedly. It becomes an admissible course of action only after other attempts to secure the unfaithful partner's repentance and reconciliation have failed.

The righteousness of Joseph, the husband of Mary

Before Joseph realized that Mary was 'with child by the Holy Spirit …, being a righteous man and not wanting to disgrace her, [he] planned to send her away secretly' (Matthew 1:18–19). Had his initial assumption about Mary been correct—that she was pregnant by another man and therefore an adulteress—Joseph, who was only engaged to her at this point, knew he had legitimate grounds for divorce. A Jewish engagement in those days was by a legal and binding contract, although the union was not to be physically consummated until after the wedding. The context suggests that because Joseph was 'a righteous man,' he at first felt he was obligated to divorce Mary. To protect her reputation, and maybe even her life, he planned to do it privately. But God wonderfully intervened and saved a marriage, while at the same time providing the promised Savior.

Jesus on what is real and ideal

Notice again what Jesus said about divorce: 'Because of your hardness of heart Moses permitted you to divorce your wives; but from the beginning it has not been this way. And I say to you, whoever divorces his wife, except for immorality, and marries another woman commits adultery'

(Matthew 19:8–9). The Greek word *skleros* has come into the English language to describe various kinds of hardening, including arteriosclerosis, hardening of the arteries. The hardness of heart Jesus decried is a total insensitivity that would lead a man to abandon 'the wife of [his] youth,' to quote Malachi 2:14, or a wife to forsake the husband with whom she made a lifetime covenant in the sight of God.

'Hardness of heart' speaks of a situation where the adultery was prolonged and the sinning spouse unrepentant, making reconciliation and a normal marriage relationship impossible. That is an important point, because in the case of a person who commits adultery but then repents, that person is showing a tenderness of heart, not hardness. That spouse is to be taken back in love. If he or she is not, then it is the other spouse who is being hard-hearted and is in danger of God's judgment. Jesus was explaining that when an adulterous husband or wife became totally insensitive to marital fidelity, God through Moses indirectly and reluctantly permitted divorce. It was a concession on account of sin to make life more bearable for the one who was sinned against.

Jesus then reminded His adversaries again of the Genesis teaching about God's intention for marriage, declaring that 'from the beginning it has not been this way' (verse 8). Divorce was never a part of God's original, ideal design for mankind.

Except for immorality

When a man obtains a divorce for any reason 'except for immorality, and marries another woman,' he commits adultery (verse 9). When giving the same basic teaching in the Sermon on the Mount, Jesus' emphasis in Matthew 5:31–32 was that the illegitimately divorced wife and her new husband would automatically become adulterers by engaging in a marriage that should never have been.

Porneia, here translated 'immorality,' is a broad term that encompasses all illicit sexual activity. In the context of marriage it always refers to adultery, which is illicit sex by a married person. The verb form of the term was used to describe the immorality for which 23,000 Israelites were killed by a plague in one day (1 Corinthians 10:8). Such wickedness threatens not only a marriage, but also the two lives represented by that marriage. Medical statistics regarding AIDS and other scourges arising from vice make that fact painfully obvious.

Although in both Matthew 5 and 19 Jesus spoke only of a man who divorces his wife, the same principle applies to a woman who divorces her husband. Our Lord did not mention that situation since it was almost unheard of among the people He initially addressed. Although a Jewish man in those days could divorce his wife on the most trivial grounds—'for any reason at all' (Matthew 19:3)—a Jewish woman could rarely divorce her husband then, even on the most serious grounds.

Jesus used the terms *immorality* and *adultery* synonymously when discussing divorce and remarriage. He emphasized that divorce that does not result *from* adultery results *in* adultery if there is remarriage.

Re-emphasizing God's graciousness

Since God is gracious to the sinning spouse by tolerating divorce instead of requiring execution, He is likewise gracious to the innocent spouse by permitting remarriage, which was permissible when a spouse died. Romans 7:2–3 says,

The married woman is bound by law to her husband while he is living; but if her husband dies, she is released from the law concerning the husband. So then, if while her husband is living she is joined to another man, she shall be called an adulteress; but if her husband dies, she is free from the law, so that she is not an adulteress though she is joined to another man [through remarriage].

How tragic for a man to make himself as good as dead to his wife through unrepentant adultery and divorce!

Yet to such a one God still shows grace. The Lord allowed that divorce to take place so that the adulterer might still have the opportunity to repent rather than be put to death, either in a temporal or eternal sense— but how grave is the peril of his or her soul every moment that person resists! In the meantime, God did not condemn the innocent one to a lifetime of singleness and loneliness that would not be required if He had the sinning partner executed. Jesus made it clear that the innocent spouse has the opportunity to again enjoy the blessings of marriage that were destroyed by the other partner's unrelenting adultery. His qualification, 'except for immorality,' clearly permits the innocent party who marries another to do so *without* committing adultery.

The final indictment

Jesus' declaration here not only reinforced His previous teaching about divorce and remarriage, but also was a devastating indictment of the Pharisees, who were then trying to devastate Him. By disregarding God's ideal for marriage, they proved guilty of proliferating adultery. May God keep our hearts tender so we never follow in their footsteps, or may He lead us to repent before Him and anyone else we've wronged if by this biblical analysis our hearts prove to be hard.

5 Is singleness the best option?

In the text we have been examining in Matthew 19, the Pharisees came out on the offensive against Jesus, using the subject of divorce as a weapon to bring Him down. Jesus masterfully rebuffed their assault, exalting God's ideal for marriage in the process, so the unrepentant Pharisees made a hasty retreat. They doubtless were thoroughly enraged, not only because they had not succeeded in making Jesus contradict Moses, but also because Jesus had succeeded in showing that they themselves were condemned by Moses in their illegitimate divorces and consequent adulteries.

The parallel text in Mark 10 tells us that after this, Jesus was alone in a house with His disciples, who began questioning Him about the whole matter again (verse 10). They may have discussed divorce and remarriage with the Lord at some length before finally saying to Him, 'If the relationship of the man with his wife is like this, it is better not to marry'—and you need to mentally supply an exclamation point to do justice to the sense of the text! Jesus said in reply,

Not all men can accept this statement, but only those to whom it has been given. For there are eunuchs who were born that way from their mother's womb; and there are eunuchs who were made eunuchs by men; and there are also eunuchs who made themselves eunuchs for the sake of the kingdom of heaven. He who is able to accept this, let him accept it (Matthew 19:10–12).

Responding to teaching far above one's upbringing

Because they had grown up in a culture where divorce was rampant, the Twelve were more than a little perplexed by what Jesus taught. Many of the Jewish people back then actually considered divorce a virtue almost on a par with marriage itself. Among the Talmudic writings of the rabbis is the statement: 'A bad wife is like leprosy to her husband. What is the remedy? Let him divorce her and be cured of his leprosy.' Even worse is: 'If a man has a bad wife, it is a religious duty to divorce her.' Such statements make no room for patience, mercy, and grace.

The difference between what the disciples had been taught all their lives and what Jesus was teaching was so radical that they were completely nonplussed. It is probable that they had looked on marriage in the same way as most of their Jewish male counterparts did—and as many people do today—believing that if things did not work out as well as they hoped, there was always divorce as an easy out. But if adultery is indeed the only divine justification for divorce, the disciples concluded, it is better not to marry.

Shallow thinking about marriage

Although their response was not well thought out, it does show that they rightly understood what Jesus was saying. They realized that the Lord was declaring marriage to be a lifetime commitment that can legitimately be broken only by death or adultery, and that even adultery does not *require* divorce. The idea of 'for better or worse' was more than they could accept. Better, they thought, not to marry at all. That exceptionally negative viewpoint is reflected by people today who say, 'I'll never get married. The last thing I want is a lifetime commitment!'

Jesus' disciples had difficulty accepting the idea of lifelong marital commitment because of the existing shallow and unbiblical view of marriage, a view that continues to inflict harm to this day. Their corrupt spiritual leaders made a practice of invalidating the Word of God for the sake of their traditions, 'teaching as doctrines the precepts of men' (Matthew 15:9). Doing the same thing today are false spiritual leaders, psychologists, sociologists, physicians, educators, librarians, and government officials—not all, but many—because of mankind's tendency to 'suppress the truth in unrighteousness' (Romans 1:18). That leads them to become 'futile in their speculations' because 'they exchanged the truth of God for a lie' (verses 21, 25). The people they influence are all too willing to believe lies and speculations instead of the Scriptures because of their own inner corruption.

Had the disciples paid more attention to God's Word than to the traditions of mere men, they would have realized that God instituted marriage as the epitome of pleasant, joyful, and fulfilling human relationships. Consider these precious truths from the Book of Proverbs alone: 'Let your fountain be blessed, and rejoice in the wife of your youth. As a loving hind and a graceful doe, let her ... satisfy you at all times; be exhilarated always with her love' (5:18–19). 'He who finds a wife finds a good thing, and obtains favor from the LORD' (18:22). 'House and wealth are an inheritance from fathers, but a prudent wife is from the LORD' (19:14).

Like most people of both sexes today, many Jewish men in New Testament times looked on marriage only as a means of gratifying their own lusts and fulfilling their own purposes. Marriage to them was little more than the socially accepted means of sexual indulgence and of procreating children. It also provided a convenient cook and housekeeper. Unlike modern people, however, most Jewish men of the day appear to have had little concern with romance.

Romance in perspective

Romance can be a beautiful part of marriage that lasts even through old age, but romantic feelings are not the basis for a sound and enduring marriage. The reason is that those feelings are largely composed of pleasant sensations toward the other person that are easily subject to change by non-moral factors such as health, age, income, or available leisure time. A sound marriage is based on permanent, unconditional commitment to one's spouse, even if romantic feelings flicker or seem extinguished because of your current circumstances. It settles into a deep friendship. That is why a pastor friend of mine always refers to his wife as his 'friend/wife.' I'm happy to tell you that I have been married for several years now, and have found that when I stop and think about my wife's faithful love toward me day in and day out, my feelings for her get a new spark. I think that is true romance, the fruit of love that doesn't quit.

If romantic feelings are the basis of a marriage, when one partner begins to lose attractiveness—and we all will to some degree since we all age—the other's attention will be turned to someone else who seems more promising and exciting. When one romantic fling after another is pursued, emotional burnout is inevitable. Such superficial relationships cannot last long and will never achieve the expected fulfillment. Each successive failure brings less satisfaction and more disappointment, disillusionment, emptiness, and loneliness. The collective result, as seen so dramatically and tragically in modern society, is a generation of disoriented, lonely, isolated, untrustworthy, untrusting, and emotionally bankrupt individuals looking for the next arousing sensation.

See beyond romance to virtue and character when selecting a mate. Be sure that you share spiritual and life values. Pursue marriage only if you both are willing to make a lifelong, one-man/one-woman, one-flesh, God-made, no-divorce union.

Real love in action after fifty years of marriage

Some years ago I heard about an elderly minister who had been married for fifty years. One morning at breakfast, his wife slumped over the table, unconscious. By the time her husband had speeded her to the hospital, she was dead. The memorial service was filled with a congregation of people grateful for the lady's love and devotion for Christ and everyone around her. After the gravesite service, the minister and his sons turned to leave. On their way home he said to his sons, 'Stop, I have to go back.' They stopped the car but said, 'Dad, we don't want you to go back. You don't need any more sorrow. We just need to move on.' He simply repeated that he needed to go back, so they did. He patted the grave, then said to his sons, 'This is a good day, a wonderful day.' When they asked what he meant, he explained, 'I know for sure that your mother is with the Lord, and I'm glad she went first. That's the way I always wanted it to be because I didn't want her to experience the grief of burying me and having to live alone.'

The minister kept serving Christ faithfully, and earned the respect of a feminist group, who decided to ask him to speak at a meeting on the subject of marriage. He wanted his listeners to understand the difference between true love as defined by the Scriptures and mere romance. After recounting his wife's death and the gratitude he felt that she died first, he said, 'Listen, any married person who knows the meaning of true love wants the other person to go first because they don't want them to endure the pain and the sorrow and the anxiety and the loneliness of burying the one they've loved. I daresay that the modern romantic relationships that try to pass for love are a far cry from that kind of feeling and that kind of reality.' He was right.

Happy commitment

Most people, including many Christians, know little of the self-giving, self-committing, and self-sacrificing love that knits two souls together for a lifetime of sharing and happiness. Instead of the rich, deepening, meaningful, and thrilling friendship that only such love can bring, they settle for a cheap, shallow substitute that fluctuates with every mood and is doomed from the beginning to be disappointing and short lived. A relationship that is built only on good feelings will soon die because those feelings originate mainly from shifting circumstances and selfish expectations. God has so designed us that a relationship built on loving commitment and self-giving concern for each other will produce emotions that not only do not die, but in fact grow richer and more satisfying with each year. Feelings are a poor foundation for a marriage, but they can be a fantastic byproduct!

The marriage based on mutual commitment is the only happy and enduring marriage. When two Christians love each other for the other's sake rather than their own and live their lives in humble submission to God's Word and to each other, a bond is formed that can withstand every temptation, disappointment, and failure that Satan and this world can hurl against them. They become lovers and friends in a way that the unbeliever and the disobedient Christian can never know.

Like the disciples, some Christians today seem afraid that lifelong, unconditional commitment will destine them to a life of boredom and frustration. They conclude with the Twelve that it is simply better not to marry. But God designed marital commitment to bring just the opposite. No marriage can be happy and satisfying—much less enduring—without it because it provides shelter and protection for love to grow, just as a family provides shelter for a baby to grow. God blesses a committed union in ways that a single person, or an uncommitted husband and wife, cannot experience and can hardly imagine. Far from being a reason to avoid marriage, lifelong and loving commitment is the very thing that makes it most fulfilling and desirable.

Choose with care

Obviously a Christian's marriage partner should be chosen carefully and with much prayer. He or she, to please God, must be 'only in the Lord' and 'believing' (1 Corinthians 7:39; 9:5). Commit yourself in marriage only to someone who shares your spiritual values and priorities. Know that there is no human joy or fulfillment that can measure up to what is experienced by the husband and wife who love Jesus Christ and each other, dwelling together in obedience to His Word in the power of His Spirit.

Cynical singleness
There is some basic biblical truth to what the disciples said about it being better not to marry, but the context suggests that it was not this truth they had in mind at the time. Their view of marriage, like that of their countrymen, focused primarily on self-centered satisfaction and fulfillment. From a gloomy utilitarian standpoint, they concluded that lonely singleness is preferable to risky marriage—as if all marriage prospects are doomed to failure at worst and disappointment at best.

Jesus, however, would not let His disciples get away with any gloom or cynicism. He approached the subject of singleness in a very honest, straightforward manner. In response to their assertion that it is better not to marry, He said,

Not all men can accept this statement, but only those to whom it has been given. For there are eunuchs who were born that way from their mother's womb; and there are eunuchs who were made eunuchs by men; and there are also eunuchs who made themselves eunuchs for the sake of the kingdom of heaven. He who is able to accept this, let him accept it (Matthew 19:11–12).

Singleness, like marriage, has its own set of problems and temptations. Not every Christian is capable of living a godly single life. First Corinthians 7:8–9 says it is good to remain single so as to be more available for ministry purposes, but that it is better to marry than to burn with lust. That is especially true for people living in societies like ours that mirror the debauchery of the Corinthian culture.

Going back to what Jesus said specifically about singleness, 'accept' conveys the idea of making room or space for something. It is a metaphor for completely embracing an idea or principle with your heart and mind so that it becomes a part of your very nature. Singleness, however, cannot be wholeheartedly accepted simply by human willpower or sincerity. Nor can it be successfully lived out simply by applying the right biblical principles. Celibate singleness is a spiritual gift according to 1 Corinthians 7. We will soon study that chapter in detail, for it is the last portion of Scripture that specifically addresses the topic of divorce and remarriage. For now, observe that it was Jesus who first said that only those who are specially gifted can spiritually survive singleness. Only those 'to whom it has been given' can find great happiness in being single and be effective in the Lord's service.

Many single Christians endure continual frustration, temptations, and unnecessary loneliness because, for one reason or another, they intentionally avoid marriage. Some are more concerned about a potential mate's appearance than his or her character. Some do not want anyone around who might invade and disrupt their selfish world. Others may be on an unrealistic quest for the perfect mate, someone who measures up in every detail to their flawed version of perfection. Others, like certain religious orders, have the mistaken belief that there is spiritual merit in celibacy and choose singleness as a means of gaining God's favor through self-sacrifice. But singleness based on any such reason dooms a person to disappointment and a lack of fulfillment. If you're beginning to think this person might be you, let me encourage you to open your heart to someone of like-precious faith in Christ and shared values. Marriage is a great gift. When two people love Jesus Christ and also love each other, sharing a life together under God's direction and in the power of the Holy Spirit, life gets so good that sometimes you have to pinch yourself to make sure it is real! That is as God intended it.

Successful singleness

Jesus described the only three categories of people who can accept singleness. First are 'eunuchs who were born that way from their mother's womb' (Matthew 19:12). These are people who are born with congenital deformities that involve undeveloped sexual capacity. Second are 'eunuchs who were made eunuchs by men,' such as the male harem guards of Jesus' day, castrated choir boys, or people who were subjected to merciless experiments during the Nazi Holocaust. Ours is a wicked world, but people who have been abused or afflicted can be very useful in God's service and enjoy great blessing.

Third are 'eunuchs who made themselves eunuchs for the sake of the kingdom of heaven.' Unlike the other two categories of people, this does not refer to a *physical* act or condition. Mutilation of the flesh to gain divine favor is a pagan idea. The Bible repudiates it. Jesus was speaking of the voluntary celibacy of those to whom that gift has been granted by God (the 'to whom it has been given' of verse 11). In that case, celibacy can indeed be 'for the sake of the kingdom of heaven' (verse 12).

The Apostle Paul had the gift of singleness and strongly exhorted others who had the gift to be content with it and to use its obvious advantages for God's glory: 'One who is unmarried is concerned about the things of the Lord, how he may please the Lord,' he said,

but one who is married is concerned about the things of the world, how he may please his wife, and his interests are divided. The woman who is unmarried, and the virgin, is concerned about the things of the Lord, that she may be holy both in body and spirit; but one who is married is concerned about the things of the world, how she may please her husband (1 Corinthians 7:32–34).

Anyone who is single can easily grasp that concept, and anyone who is married already knows it is true by experience.

Accepting the whole package of God's truth about relationships

'He who is able to accept this, let him accept it,' said Jesus. In the narrowest sense, He was saying that those who by God's gifting are able to accept a life of celibate singleness should accept it as God's will for them. In a broader sense, He seems to have been making a concluding statement about the whole topic under discussion. Jesus wanted His disciples to accept everything He had just taught about marriage, divorce, remarriage, and singleness. That is what He wants of His disciples today.

Jesus wants us to put aside the false ideas and practices we have inherited from humanly devised and unscriptural traditions. He wants us to accept His Word and live accordingly. People who are not Christians cannot accept Jesus' standards for marriage and divorce, and would not have the resources to live up to those standards even if they did. The idea of self-giving, unconditional, and lifelong commitment in any area of life, including marriage, runs completely against the grain of fallen human nature. Only those who honor Jesus as Lord and Savior can truly accept His teachings. Are you willing to do that now if you haven't already?

6 Marriage in a troubled society

First Corinthians 7 is a particularly practical section of Scripture. It marks the beginning of the Apostle Paul's specific answers to questions that were troubling the believers in Corinth. Their first questions were about marriage, an area in which the Corinthians had serious problems. Much of their marital trouble reflected the pagan and morally corrupt society in which they lived and from which they had not fully separated. Their society tolerated fornication, adultery, homosexuality, polygamy, concubines, women's liberation movements, and multiple marriages and divorces. Does that sound somewhat familiar? Because we have our own set of questions to ask about divorce, remarriage, and living out God's ideal for marriage, after we study how God inspired Paul to answer the Corinthian church's questions, we will conclude with a question-and-answer section that endeavors to shed biblical light on any of our own practical concerns that remain.

Four types of marriage under Roman law

In New Testament times, four types of marriage were practiced under Roman law. The first was called *contubernium*, which means 'tent companionship.' It was administered by slave owners, who generally treated their slaves like subhuman chattels. If a man and woman slave wanted to be married, their owner might allow them to live together in this first state. The arrangement lasted only as long as the owner permitted. The owner was tragically free to separate them, to arrange for other partners, or to sell one or the other. Many of the early Christians were slaves, and some of them had lived—perhaps were still living—in this basic sort of marital relationship. Although the blight of slavery still exists in some parts of the world, it is rare. What is common today with the world of the Corinthians is lots of live-in sex, which is basically what the *contubernium* legislated.

A second type of marriage was called *usus*, a form of what we call common-law marriage, which recognized a couple as husband and wife after they had lived together for a year. We have situations like that today where a man and woman have lived together long enough to have several children together, but have never legally married.

A third type was the *coemptio in manum*, in which a father would sell his daughter to a prospective husband. Such arrangements still occur today. A man who became a new believer told me about a wife his family purchased for him in the Orient. He didn't like her, so he took off for America. After six years, he became a Christian and wanted to know what God wanted him to do about her. Such matters were daily issues in the Corinthian church. Perhaps you are beginning to understand why people in New Testament times had serious questions about marriage. Be encouraged that since God provided answers for them, His Word can certainly help us with our marriage problems.

The fourth type of marriage under the Roman Empire was much more elevated than the previous three. Members of the Patrician class, the nobility, were married in a service called the *confarreatio*, on which the modern Christian marriage ceremony is based. It was adopted by the Roman Catholic Church in medieval times and used with certain Christian modifications—coming, with little change, into Protestantism through the Reformation. The original ceremony involved participation by both families in the arrangements for the wedding, a matron to accompany the bride and a man to accompany the bridegroom, the exchanging of vows, the wearing of a veil by the bride, the giving of a ring (placed on the third finger of the left hand), a bridal bouquet, and a wedding cake.

Cutting through the confusion

In the Roman Empire of Paul's day, divorce was common, even among those married under the noble *confarreatio*. Juvenal, the Roman poet (AD 60–140), wrote satires of women who wore out their bridal veils with so many marriages. It was not unheard of for women and men to have been married twenty times or more. One of the reasons was an active and vocal feminist movement during this time. Some wives competed with their husbands in business and even in feats of physical strength. Many were not interested in being housewives and mothers, so by the end of the first century, childless marriages were common. Both men and women were determined to live their own lives, regardless of marriage vows or commitments.

The early church had members who had lived together, and were still living together, under all four marriage arrangements. It also included those who had multiple marriages and divorces. Because of the notorious immorality of their city, some believers in Corinth had gotten the notion that being single and celibate was more spiritual than being married, so they disparaged marriage entirely. There was in Corinth the Temple of Aphrodite, which had at least 1,000 priestesses who would descend each night into the streets of Corinth to ply their trade as religious prostitutes. Coming out of that extreme background, some Christians wrongly concluded that sex is unspiritual and should be avoided completely. That view still exists to this day, and will get worse: Paul warned that in the last days before Christ returns, false teachers will 'forbid marriage and advocate abstaining from foods which God has created to be gratefully shared in by those who believe and know the truth' (1 Timothy 4:3). It is a great evil to denounce God's good gifts, one of which is marriage.

The marital situation in Corinth was difficult and perplexing, even for mature Christians. For the immature Corinthians it was especially confusing. The great question was, 'What do we do now that we are believers? Should we stay together as husband and wife if we are both Christians? Should we get a divorce if our spouses are unbelievers? Should we try to get back together with partners long gone before our conversion to Christ? Should we become, or remain, single?' The chaos of marital possibilities posed myriad perplexities, which Paul answered in 1 Corinthians 7. The first seven verses address the issue of celibacy. Paul made it clear that celibacy is good, that it can be tempting, that it is wrong for married people, and that it is a gift from God. The main emphasis throughout the chapter is on the sanctity of both marriage and singleness.

Celibacy is good, but not superior to marriage

'Now concerning the things about which you wrote,' begins verse 1, 'it is good for a man not to touch a woman.' That is not referring to a mere touch. When I was a high-school student going on a church youth-group activity, a well-meaning but misguided chaperon used that verse as justification for insisting that the boys and the girls go on separate hayrides! Later, I learned that 'to touch a woman' was a common Jewish euphemism for sexual intercourse. The phrase was used in that sense in Genesis 20:6 and Ruth 2:9, for example, to describe how Sarah and Ruth were protected from sexual sin. Paul was using it to state that it is a good thing for Christians not to have sexual intercourse, that is, to be unmarried. He did not say, however, that singleness is the only good condition or that marriage is in any way wrong or inferior to singleness. He said only that singleness, as long as it is celibate, can be a good thing.

God Himself declared at creation that 'it is not good for the man to be alone; I will make him a helper suitable for him' (Genesis 2:18). All people need companionship, and God ordained marriage to be, among other things, the most fulfilling and common means of companionship. Marriage is not the only form of companionship, however. God gives us good friends and He 'sets the solitary in families' (Psalm 68:6, New King James Version).

God allowed for singleness and did not require marriage for everyone, but Jewish tradition came to look upon marriage as the ideal state, regarding singleness as disobedience to God's command to 'Be fruitful and multiply, and fill the earth' (Genesis 1:28). That is to make an idol out of marriage, which is an affront to God, the maker of marriage. Jesus corrected that serious error when He said, 'In the resurrection they neither marry nor are given in marriage, but are like angels in heaven' (Matthew 22:30), meaning that marriage is only for this life. Redeemed, resurrected mankind will relate to one another on a higher, broader level of love than marriage, in a way similar to that by which angelic beings relate to one another now in heaven.

Because of their cultural baggage, Jewish Christians in Corinth may have been pressuring single Gentile believers to become married. Some of the Gentiles, on the other hand, perhaps because of past experiences they had had, were inclined to remain single. Just as the Jews had done with marriage, those Gentiles, reacting to the sexual sin of their past, came to look on celibacy not only as the ideal state, but also as the only truly godly state. Scripture affirms neither of those extremes. Paul acknowledged that singleness is good, honorable, and excellent, but he did not support the claim that it is a more spiritual state or that it is more acceptable to God than marriage.

Celibacy is tempting, but marriage is not a mere escape valve

After affirming the value of singleness, Paul gave this caution: 'But because of immoralities, each man is to have his own wife, and each woman is to have her own husband' (1 Corinthians 7:2). That does not imply that every Corinthian church member was immoral, although many of them were. Paul was speaking in general of the danger of fornication for those who are single. Because sexual desire is unfulfilled and can be very strong, there is great temptation to sexual immorality for those who are not married, especially in societies—such as that of ancient Rome and our own—where sexual sin is freely practiced and glorified.

Marriage, however, cannot be reduced simply to being God's escape valve for the sex drive. Paul was not suggesting that Christians go out and find another Christian to marry only to keep from getting into moral sin. He taught a much higher view of marriage than that; for example, his wonderful description in Ephesians 5 of a man's love for his wife as a picture of Christ's love for His church. Marriage is not an end in itself, existing only for our happiness and fulfillment, but is primarily an illustration on a human level of a divine relationship. We can't expect worldly people to understand that, but we certainly can expect the church to. Paul's purpose in 1 Corinthians 7, however, was to stress the reality of the sexual temptations of singleness and to acknowledge that they have a legitimate outlet in marriage. That is why he wrote, 'Each man is to have his own wife, and each woman is to have her own husband' (verse 2). I love that word 'own' here. It speaks volumes about personal contentment with God's particular provision for our most personal needs.

Scriptural reasons for marriage

Scripture gives us several reasons for marriage. First, *marriage is for procreation*. God commanded Adam and Eve to 'be fruitful and multiply' (Genesis 1:28). Mankind is to reproduce itself. Specifically, God intends for husbands and wives together to cherish and personally nurture each precious child with which He entrusts them. Second, *marriage is for pleasure*. Recall the Proverbs text that speaks of a man's being 'exhilarated always' with the wife of his youth (5:18–19). Also, as we will soon see specifically, the Song of Solomon rejoices in the physical attractions and pleasures of marital love. A discreet yet joyful translation of Genesis 26:8,

'Isaac was sporting with Rebekah his wife' (King James Version), conveys the pleasure aspect of marriage. Third, *marriage is a partnership*. Woman was created for man to be 'a helper suitable for him' (Genesis 2:18). Cooperation between husband and wife is one of the key ingredients of a good marriage. You'll find that God is such a perfect matchmaker that where one partner is weak, the other is strong, so they help each other glorify God to a much higher degree than they ever could alone. Fourth, *marriage is a picture of the church*, as we learned from Ephesians 5. The husband is to have authority over and to love his wife just as Christ has authority over and loves His church (verses 23–32). Fifth, *marriage is for provision*. Ephesians 5 also teaches that the husband is to nourish and cherish his wife, caring for her needs as consistently as he does for his own needs. And sixth, *marriage is for purity*. It protects from sexual immorality by meeting the need for physical fulfillment. Although celibacy is good, it is not superior to marriage, and it has dangers and temptations that marriage does not have.

Celibacy is wrong for married people

Imagine how foolish it would be to strip marriage of its protection from sexual temptation. That is the sense of Paul's instruction in 1 Corinthians 7:3–5:

The husband must fulfill his duty to his wife, and likewise also the wife to her husband. The wife does not have authority over her own body, but the husband does; and likewise also the husband does not have authority over his own body, but the wife does. Stop depriving one another, except by agreement for a time, so that you may devote yourselves to prayer, and come together again so that Satan will not tempt you because of your lack of self-control.

That celibacy is wrong for those who are married should be an obvious truth, but it was not obvious to some of the Corinthian believers. Because of their erroneous belief in the spiritual superiority of total sexual abstinence, more than a few members in the church practiced it even within marriage. Some overzealous husbands apparently had decided to set themselves apart wholly for God. In doing so, however, they neglected or even denied their responsibilities to their wives, especially in the area of sexual relations. Some wives had done the same thing. The practice of deprivation probably was most common when the spouse was not a believer, but as we will see, Paul applied his command to all marriages. Married believers are not to sexually deprive their spouses, whether the spouse is a Christian or not.

Intimate mutual obligations

The apostle made no exception to the instruction that the husband fulfill his duty to his wife, and likewise also the wife to her husband. God holds all marriage to be sacred, and He holds sexual relations between husband and wife to be not only sacred but also proper and even obligatory. His Word makes it clear that physical relations within marriage are not simply a privilege and a pleasure, but also a responsibility. Husbands and wives have a special duty to give sexual satisfaction to each other. There is no distinction between the sexual needs of men and women. The husband has no more rights in this regard than the wife.

Notice how Paul reinforced the mutuality of obligation: 'The wife does not have authority over her own body, but the husband does; and likewise also the husband does not have authority over his own body, but the wife does' (verse 4). God honors sexual desire and expression within marriage. It was His idea in the first place. In fact, failure for Christian husbands and wives to submit sexually to the authority of their spouses brings dishonor to God because it dishonors marriage.

The present tense of the verb translated 'have authority over' indicates a general statement that is always true. Spouses' mutual authority over each other's body is continuous; it lasts throughout their marriage. In one sense, a Christian's body is his or her own to take care of and to use as a gift from God. In the deepest spiritual sense, it belongs entirely to God. But in the marital realm, it also belongs to the marriage partner.

Sexual expression within marriage is not an option or an extra. It is certainly not, as it has sometimes been considered, a necessary evil in which spiritual Christians engage only to procreate children. It is far more than a physical act. God created sex to be the expression and experience of love on the deepest human level, forging a beautiful and powerful bond between husband and wife.

Physical joy in marriage

The best illustration of the physical joy of marriage is in the Song of Solomon. You will never find more magnificent lyrics. Listen to what the husband says:

How beautiful you are, my darling,
How beautiful you are!
Your eyes are like doves behind your veil ...
Your lips are like a scarlet thread,
And your mouth is lovely ...
You are altogether beautiful, my darling,
And there is no blemish in you ...
You have made my heart beat faster, my sister, my bride ...
with a single glance of your eyes ...
How much better is your love than wine! (Song of Solomon 4:1, 3, 7, 9–10).

Wouldn't you like to hear that, ladies? I wish I could think of things like that to say to my wife more often!

The wife is equally thrilled: 'My beloved is dazzling and ruddy, outstanding among ten thousand ... His mouth is full of sweetness. And he is wholly desirable. This is my beloved and this is my friend' (5:10, 16). Then she cries out, 'I am my beloved's, and his desire is for me' (7:10). In the *coup de grâce* she says, 'He has brought me to his banquet hall, and his banner over me is love. Sustain me with raisin cakes, refresh me with apples, because I am lovesick' (2:4–5). She is really excited about this guy! Her husband feels the same way about her, and that is how marriage ought to be. God designed marriage to be an arena for expressing love. He created and honors sexual desire in marriage, 'a bold and blessed intoxication,' as it has been called. God intends for marriage and the sexual relationship within it to be lifelong and mutually satisfying.

It is no wonder, then, that Paul was so adamant that married couples not forsake their sexual relationship: 'Stop depriving one another' (1 Corinthians 7:5) is an emphatic command. Sexual relations between a husband and his wife are God ordained and commanded.

66

An exception both mutual and temporary for devotion

The exception Paul gave under the inspiration of the Holy Spirit is both mutual and temporary: 'by agreement for a time, so that you may devote yourselves to prayer' (verse 5). If both partners agree to abstain from sexual activity for a brief period to allow one or both of them to spend time in intensive prayer, they may do so. The length of time for physical separation and the specific need and purpose of the prayer are to be agreed on in advance. God may give us a strong burden about a person or a ministry, a burden that requires our undivided attention and concentrated prayer. Grief or serious illness, for example, may lead to this. Another example is if—God forbid—we become ensnared in sin and need to withdraw for a set period of time to get straightened out with the Lord, our spouse, and anyone else we have wounded.

We find a biblical example of brief marital abstention before the Lord God came down to Mount Sinai to manifest Himself in great power and glory. In preparation for His awesome coming, the Israelites were to consecrate themselves, wash their clothes, and abstain from sexual relations. Moses said to the people, 'Be ready for the third day; do not go near a woman' (Exodus 19:15).

Hundreds of years later, in response to His people's extreme wickedness, the Lord God commanded,

'Return to Me with all your heart,
And with fasting, weeping, and mourning;
And rend your heart and not your garments.'
Now return to the LORD your God ...
Who knows whether He will not turn and relent ...
Gather the people, sanctify the congregation,
Assemble the elders,
Gather the children and the nursing infants.
Let the bridegroom come out of his room
And the bride out of her bridal chamber (Joel 2:12–16).

The need for forgiveness was so pressing that even those who were just married were to leave their nuptial chambers to join in national mourning and repentance.

In the future, when our Lord Jesus Christ returns, He will 'pour out on the house of David and on the inhabitants of Jerusalem, the Spirit of grace and of supplication, so that they will look on [Him] whom they have pierced; and they will mourn for Him … The land will mourn, every family by itself; the family of the house of David by itself and their wives by themselves' (Zechariah 12:10–12). Marriage relations will be set aside during that awesome time of mourning and spiritual restoration—truly a prophetic zenith.

Not being taken advantage of by the devil

When such urgent spiritual needs are past, normal marital relations are to resume. Husbands and wives are then to 'come together again' (1 Corinthians 7:5). The reason for coming back together is explicit in the rest of the verse: 'so that Satan will not tempt you because of your lack of self-control.' When the time of concentrated prayer is over, normal desires and temptations will return, often with greater intensity. Satan knows that God's people can be especially vulnerable after a mountaintop experience, and as God's arch-enemy, he would love to take advantage of the situation. Our defenses are apt to be down and our pride may be up. Or, because of the experience, we may simply not have the desire for sex awhile afterward. Our spouse, on the other hand, especially if he or she has not shared in the prayer, may have developed a particularly strong desire during the separation. As a guard against falling into temptation ourselves, or of causing our marriage partner to fall into temptation, sexual relations are to resume immediately.

This is serious enough to bear repeating: Unless it is by mutual consent, for a specific prayer need, and for a brief period, sexual abstinence within marriage can become a tool of Satan. Plan your married life together accordingly. Abstention is never to be used as a pretense of spiritual superiority or as a means of intimidating or manipulating your spouse. Physical love is to be a normal and regular experience shared by both marriage partners alike, viewed as the wonderful gift from God that it is.

Spirituality is not determined by marital status

Paul's next comment in answer to the Corinthians' questions about marriage seems puzzling at first glance: 'But this I say by way of concession, not of command. Yet I wish that all men were even as I myself am. However, each man has his own gift from God, one in this manner, and another in that' (1 Corinthians 7:6–7). I do not believe 'concession' is the best translation of the Greek term *sungnomē*, which means to think the same thing as someone, to have a joint opinion, a common understanding, or an awareness of something. 'But this I say' refers back to what Paul was just saying about how marriage protects the majority of Christian men and women from sexual sin. I think Paul was saying that he was aware of the goodness of being single and celibate, yet aware also of the benefits and responsibilities of marriage. He wanted to make sure his comments were not misunderstood as a command for every believer to be married.

Marriage was instituted by God as the norm for man–woman relationships. As such it is a great blessing to mankind. It is not required for believers or anyone else, however. Paul's point is this: If you are single, that is good; if you are married or get married, stay married and retain normal marital relations, for that is of God. Spirituality is not determined by marital status.

Singleness and marriage are both special gifts

In one sense, Paul wished that all believers could be single, even as he himself was. He surely had in mind the great freedom he had as a single person to serve Christ—and who indeed has been more fruitful in Christian service than Paul? But Paul did not expect all believers to be unmarried. He did not expect all who were then single to stay single. And for those who were already married, it would be wrong for them to live as if they were single, to become celibate while married.

Although celibacy is good for Christians who are not married, it is a gift from God that He does not give to every believer. Just as it is wrong to misuse a gift that we have, so it is wrong to try to use a gift that we don't have. For a person who does not have the gift of celibacy, trying to practice it brings moral and spiritual frustration. But for those who have it as God's gift, singleness—like all His gifts—is a great blessing.

The attitude about singleness among most professing Christians today, however, is often like that of the Jewish majority in Paul's day. It is looked down on as a second-class condition by some, and others go so far as to assume that something must be *wrong* with a single man or woman. 'Not so,' said Paul, under the inspiration of the Holy Spirit. If singleness is God's gift to a person, it is God's will for that person to accept and exercise the gift. It won't be a chore to do so because the gift of singleness is being single and loving it. The gift is being single and not being tempted on a regular basis (it may happen once in a while). The gift is being single and not being preoccupied with being single. If people so gifted are submissive to God, they will live in singleness all their days in contentment, happiness, and spiritual usefulness.

Rachel Saint served as a single missionary among the Waodani Indians of Ecuador for many years. She poured out her life and her love to the Indians, and found great blessing and fulfillment. In like manner, so have many other choice servants of Christ, comprising a great honor roll in heaven. Part of the fun of eternity will be learning their stories and swapping them with ours.

Singleness has many practical advantages. It allows much greater freedom in where and how a person serves the Lord. A single person is freer to move around and set his or her own hours and schedule. If God has given you the ability to be single, cherish that ability because of its lack of encumbrance. Married persons have many cares and concerns that the unmarried do not have (1 Corinthians 7:32–34), as we noted in our study of Matthew 19, where Jesus described singleness as a gift only for 'those to whom it has been given' (verse 11). Both Jesus and Paul made it clear that the celibate life is not God's preferred state for all believers, but only for those specially gifted.

'Each man has his own gift from God, one in this manner [singleness], and another in that [marriage],' said Paul in conclusion (1 Corinthians 7:7). Our purpose as Christians is to discover the gifts God has given us and to use those gifts faithfully and joyfully in His service, without either envying or disparaging the gifts we do not have.

7 Divine guidelines for singleness and marriage

In the United States and many other countries around the world, almost every other marriage ends in divorce. There are nearly as many divorces as marriages each year. Love today is loudly acclaimed and sought after, but it is not much evident—even within marriages.

Marriage problems are not unique to modern times. They have occurred throughout history, and were rampant in New Testament times under the Roman Empire. As we have been studying, the church in Corinth was severely afflicted. The Corinthian believers were hurting, so they wrote Paul with a list of practical questions. His answers in 1 Corinthians 7:1–7 establish the general principle that marriage is the norm for Christians, but that singleness as a special gift of God is good. In verses 8–16 we see that basic truth applied to four groups of believers: (1) Christians who were previously married; (2) Christians married to other Christians; (3) Christians married to non-Christians content to stay married; (4) Christians married to non-Christians who want to leave the marriage.

Options for single Christians

In the Book of 1 Corinthians we have preserved for our benefit answers to a variety of spiritual questions, but we do not know exactly how the questions were worded. Clearly one of them was, 'Should those who were married and divorced before becoming Christians remarry?' Formerly-married people came to salvation in Christ and asked if they now had the right to marry someone else. Paul's response in verses 8–9 is uniquely fitted to those who want to know their options: 'I say to the unmarried and to widows that it is good for them if they remain even as I. But if they do not have self-control, let them marry; for it is better to marry than to burn with passion.'

The unmarried and widows are the two categories of single people mentioned here, but there is a third category of single people mentioned in verse 25: 'virgins.' Understanding the distinctions between those three groups is essential to understanding and obeying God's instructions. Virgins (*parthenoi*) are single people who have never been married. Widows (*chērais*) are single people who formerly were married, but were severed from that relationship by the death of the spouse. That leaves the matter of the unmarried. Who are they?

The term translated 'unmarried' is *agamos*, which comes from the word translated 'marriage' or 'wedding' with the negative prefix *a*. It is used only four times in the New Testament, and all four are in 1 Corinthians 7. We need not go elsewhere to understand this key term. Verse 32 uses it in a way that gives little hint about its specific meaning; it simply refers to a person who is not married. Verse 34 uses it more definitively: 'the woman who is unmarried, and the virgin.' Paul obviously had two distinct groups in mind, so whoever the unmarried are, they are not virgins. Verse 8 speaks 'to the unmarried and to widows,' so we can conclude that the unmarried are not widows. The last use of the term, in verses 10–11, gives us the clearest picture: 'The wife should not leave her husband (but if she does leave, she must remain unmarried).' The unmarried woman here is a divorced woman.

A specific word to divorced people

Paul was speaking to people who were divorced before coming to Christ. They wanted to know if they had the right to marry. Here is the answer: 'It is good for them if they remain even as I [single]. But if they do not have self-control, let them marry; for it is better to marry than to burn with passion ... Brethren, each one is to remain with God in that condition in which he was called' (verses 8–9, 24). People who have a divorce in their past before the Lord called them to Himself may leave that divorce in their past. There is no reason for salvation to change anyone's marital status. Paul later wrote the Corinthians another time, explaining, 'If anyone is in Christ, he is a new creature; the old things passed away; behold, new things have come' (2 Corinthians 5:17). Do not seek to dredge up old marital ties. It is time for new options: remaining single if you are so gifted or getting married to a fellow Christian if you are not.

Paul's first option to those who are now free of marriage is 'that it is good for them if they remain even as I' (1 Corinthians 7:8). By that statement Paul affirmed that he was formerly married. Marriage seems to have been required for membership in the Sanhedrin, the Jewish ruling council, to which Paul may have once belonged because of this testimony, among other evidences, 'I was advancing in Judaism beyond many of my contemporaries among my countrymen, being more extremely zealous for my ancestral traditions' (Galatians 1:14). It is likely that Paul was a widower. He did not identify himself with the virgins but with the unmarried and widows, that is, with the formerly married.

People who are single when they come to Christ should know it is good for them to stay that way. There is no need to rush into marriage. Many well-meaning Christians, however, are not content to let them remain single. The urge to play matchmaker can be strong, but mature believers must resist it. Marriage is not necessary or superior to singleness.

Anna, the joyful widow

One of the most beautiful stories associated with Jesus' birth and infancy is that of Anna. When Mary and Joseph brought the baby Jesus to the Temple to present Him to the Lord and offer a sacrifice, the prophetess Anna recognized Jesus as the promised Messiah. At the very moment the prophet Simeon finished testifying of Jesus as the Christ or Messiah, 'she came up and began giving thanks to God, and continued to speak of Him to all those who were looking for the redemption of Jerusalem' (Luke 2:38). The Scriptures tell us that Anna's husband had lived only seven years after their marriage, and she had since remained a widow. At the age of eighty-four she was still faithfully serving the Lord in His Temple, serving day and night with fasting and prayers. She did not look on her lot as inferior and certainly not as meaningless. She had the gift of singleness and used it joyfully in the Lord's work. If you are a widow or widower, God may choose for you never to marry again. If He gives you the gift to be satisfied and at peace with yourself as a single person, accept that from His hand and use it for His glory.

When passion turns to flame

Remaining single is a great option for Christians who use their singleness for godly purposes, as Anna did, but honesty is required. They need to go before the Lord in prayer and ask Him to help them search their hearts. If they find 'they do not have self-control, let them marry,' said Paul, explaining that 'it is better to marry than to burn with passion' (1 Corinthians 7:9). If a Christian is single but does not have the gift of singleness and is being strongly tempted sexually on a regular basis, he or she should pursue marriage. 'Let them marry' translates a Greek aorist imperative, indicating a strong command. God knows it is difficult for a person to serve Him if he or she is continually burning with sexual desire—even if the desire never results in actual immorality. He cares about all our needs, and makes provision for them. In a society such as Corinth's, or ours, in which immorality is so prevalent and accepted, He realizes it is especially difficult not to succumb to temptation. Nevertheless, 'no temptation has overtaken you but such as is common to man; and God is faithful, who will not allow you to be tempted beyond what you are able, but with the temptation will provide the way of escape also, so that you will be able to endure it' (1 Corinthians 10:13). Marriage is one of His provisions. If it is God's will for you to be married, He will provide a spouse in His perfect timing. If it is not His will, He will give you grace to live a single life. Either way, keep Him at the center of your hopes, desires, and ambitions, and trust Him in the outworking of His providence.

Keeping your engagement period short

I believe that once a Christian couple decides to get married, they should do it as soon as reasonable, and carefully limit the amount of time they spend alone together before the wedding. In a day of lowered standards, careless self-expression, and constant suggestiveness, it is difficult to stay sexually pure when faced with the opportunity for intimacy with the one to whom you've pledged yourself. The practical problems of an early marriage are not nearly as serious as the danger of immorality when your guard is down during this very tempting time in your life, as you await the imminent fulfillment that your marriage will bring.

When waiting for marriage prospects

Taking the option of marriage is obviously more difficult for the person who has strong sexual desires but no immediate prospects for a husband or wife. It is never God's will for Christians to marry unbelievers, but neither is it right just to marry the first believer who will say yes. Although we may want very much to be married, we should be careful. Strong feelings of any sort tend to dull judgment and make us vulnerable and careless.

If you are a Christian in this dilemma, there are several things you ought to do. First, do not simply seek to be married. Don't take any plane that's leaving the airport: Figure out where you want to go before you get on! Seek to honor Christ in your life and relationships, leaving it to God to bring about a marriage with someone who also is seeking to honor Christ. He will lead you to someone you can love, trust, and respect. It may help you most to think of it this way: *Seek to love and let marriage come as a response in God's own time.*

Second, it is fine to be on the lookout for the right person, but realize that the only way to *find* the right person is to *be* the right person. Instead of being preoccupied with the right woman, start being the right man. Instead of being preoccupied with the right man, start being the right woman. Then the right man will recognize the right woman! If two believers are right with God and it is His will for them to be married, He will bring them together—and never too late.

Third, cultivate friendships with mature Christians who understand your needs and will hold you accountable. Pray often for each other and study the Scriptures together. Avoid living and traveling alone when you can do otherwise.

Fourth, redirect your energy in ways that will be most helpful in keeping your mind off temptation and onto God and His Word. Two of the best ways are spiritual service and physical activity. Idle moments don't help at all. Be proactive in not listening to, looking at, or being around anything that strengthens sexual temptation. Philippians 4:8 explains what to do instead: 'Whatever is *true*, whatever is *honorable*, whatever is *right*, whatever is *pure*, whatever is *lovely*, whatever is of *good repute*, if there is any *excellence* and if anything worthy of *praise*, dwell on these things' (emphasis added). Never be preoccupied with what you *can't* do but with what you *can*, by God's grace. Here are verses that will help you tremendously during this season in your life if you take them to heart: Present your body as 'a living and holy sacrifice, acceptable to God, which is your spiritual service of worship. And do not be conformed to this world, but be transformed by the renewing of your mind, so that you may prove what the will of God is, that which is good and acceptable and perfect' (Romans 12:1–2).

Fifth, realize that, until God gives you the right person to be your mate in His perfect time, He will provide strength to resist temptation. Remember and believe the promise of 1 Corinthians 10:13, that He will not allow His children to be tempted beyond what they can bear.

Finally, if you truly believe that, you will find yourself saying with Paul, 'I have learned to be content in whatever circumstances I am … I can do all things through Him who strengthens me' (Philippians 4:11, 13). Be content with your singleness to the point that you can sincerely praise God for it—even if singleness turns out to be His permanent plan for you. Praise has a very wholesome effect. You will find your relationship with God deepening as you sense Him personally ministering to your deepest needs.

Guidelines for Christians married to other Christians

Turning back to Paul's instructions in 1 Corinthians 7, here is what he wrote to Christians married to other Christians: 'To the married I give instructions, not I, but the Lord, that the wife should not leave her husband (but if she does leave, she must remain unmarried, or else be reconciled to her husband), and that the husband should not divorce his wife' (verses 10–11). No distinction is made regarding the type of marriage involved, ranging from the common-law *usus* to the noble *confarreatio*, which we discussed in the previous chapter. 'To the married' covers every type—then and now. That both partners of the marriage in view here were and are Christians is clear from Paul's giving them 'instructions'—something he never gave unbelievers—and because verses 12–16 deal specifically with marriages in which only one partner is a believer. God's main instruction to married believers is to stay together. Why? To prove themselves true to each other, to love each other, and to make everything of that marriage that God designed it to be.

Paul made clear the source of his teaching by adding, 'not I, but the Lord.' It was his way of signaling a direct quotation, which is even clearer than our modern use of quotation marks. He highlighted Jesus' emphasis in Matthew 5 and 19 that divorce is contrary to God's plan for mankind, as we studied in Chapters 1–5 of this book. Paul here was not discussing divorce based on adultery, for which Jesus specifically affirmed provision. He was talking about divorce for other reasons, even supposedly spiritual ones.

We do not know why some of the Corinthian Christians wanted to divorce their partners. In light of 1 Corinthians 7:1–7, it is likely that some church members thought they could live holier and more dedicated lives as celibates and wanted to divorce for that reason. The majority probably wanted to leave their mates for fleshly reasons. *Whatever* the reasons, Christians are not to divorce other Christians: 'The wife should not leave her husband' and 'the husband should not divorce his wife' (verses 10–11). The terms translated 'leave' and 'divorce' ('put away' in some translations), in the context of man–woman relationships, always mean divorce, and such action is forbidden to Christian couples.

These are the Lord's commands

Some of the believers in Corinth had already divorced each other or were in motion toward that tragic end. To a Christian woman (or man) in that situation, God's instructions are: 'If she does leave, she must remain unmarried, or else be reconciled to her husband' (verse 11). If a Christian does divorce another Christian, except for adultery, neither partner is given freedom from the Lord to marry someone else. They must remain single or come back together as man and wife. In God's eyes, that union has never been broken.

What I am writing here is not my opinion as a pastor or a counselor; these are the Lord's commands. Take heart, though: Just as God is faithful to help those who are longing to be married, so He will help those who are longing for solutions to their marriage problems. The help and close fellowship with God come to all who will trust and obey Him. If you are married to a Christian, He wants you to stay married. If you have already violated that command, for God's sake stop there and don't go any further. Either be reconciled with your Christian spouse or else stay single the rest of your life. God knows that having only those two options will motivate His people to depend on Him to make their marriages last. He will never disappoint those who put their trust in Him.

Guidelines for Christians married to unbelievers who want to stay

Just as Paul made it clear when he was directly quoting the Lord Jesus, he likewise made it clear when he was not:

To the rest I say, not the Lord, that if any brother has a wife who is an unbeliever, and she consents to live with him, he must not divorce her. If any woman has a husband who is an unbeliever, and he consents to live with her, she should not divorce him. For the unbelieving husband is sanctified through his wife, and the unbelieving wife is sanctified through her believing husband; for otherwise your children are unclean, but now they are holy (verses 12–14, a blend of the New American and English Standard translations).

That text answers several questions: What were Christians to do who were already married to unbelievers, especially immoral and idolatrous ones? Were they exposing themselves and their children to a hopelessly corrupting influence? Were they free to get a divorce and then either live singly or marry a fellow Christian?

Those are all fair questions. In the previous chapter of 1 Corinthians, we read: 'Flee immorality. Every other sin that a man commits is outside the body, but the immoral man sins against his own body. Or do you not know that your body is a temple of the Holy Spirit who is in you, whom you have from God, and that you are not your own? For you have been bought with a price: therefore glorify God in your body' (6:18–20). Second Corinthians 6:14–15 says, 'Do not be bound together with unbelievers; for what partnership have righteousness and lawlessness, or what fellowship has light with darkness? Or what harmony has Christ with [Satan]?' The Corinthians were not the only Christians to have feared that their being married to unbelievers was like joining Christ to Satan, defiling the believer and any children involved, and deeply dishonoring to the Lord Himself. Whether saddled with such fears or not, any Christian married to a non-Christian will have trouble, so the desire to have a Christian partner instead can be a very strong temptation.

Since Jesus had not taught directly about that problem, Paul said, 'To the rest I say, not the Lord' (1 Corinthians 7:12). That is not a denial of divine inspiration, or an indication that Paul was merely giving his own opinion. God had not given any previous revelation on that subject but now, through Paul, the apostle to the Gentiles, He set it forth to help His growing church.

The power to sanctify a home

Christians married to unbelievers are not to worry that they themselves, their marriage, or their children will be defiled by the unbelieving spouse. On the contrary, the opposite is true: Both the children and the unbelieving spouse are sanctified through the believing wife or husband (verse 14). For the non-Christian husband, it would be just as if his wife received a huge inheritance: He had nothing to do with it and is not related to the benefactor, but he still gets to cash in. He is not related to God, but he gets to enjoy benefits that God is pouring out on his wife. Christian, if your partner wants to stay, let him or her stay and experience the blessing of God.

Being unequally yoked with an unbeliever will be frustrating, discouraging, and even painful at times, but it need not be defiling because even one believer has the power to sanctify an entire household. The sanctification in verse 14 does not refer to salvation; otherwise, the spouse would not be spoken of as unbelieving. It refers to being set apart, which is the basic meaning of the Greek words translated 'sanctify' and 'holy,' terms that come from the same Greek root. This sanctification is matrimonial and familial, not personal or spiritual. In God's eyes, a home is set apart for Himself when the husband, wife, or (by implication) any other family member is a Christian. Such a home is not Christian in the full sense, but it is immeasurably superior to one that is totally unbelieving. Even if the Christian is ridiculed and persecuted, unbelievers in the family are blessed because of that believer, especially by being exposed to biblical truth. One Christian in a home graces the entire home. God's indwelling of that believer and all the blessings and graces that flow into the believer's life from heaven will spill over to enrich all who are near.

In addition, although the believer's faith cannot suffice for the salvation of anyone but him- or herself, the believer is often the means of other family members coming to the Lord by the power of his or her testimony.

A young woman came up to me after the service one Sunday morning and told me that when she was growing up, her grandmother was the only Christian in the family. The grandmother spoke freely of her love for Christ and witnessed to the family by what she did as well as by what she said. Eventually, three of the four grandchildren came to know the Lord, and all declared that their grandmother had the greatest influence on their decision for Christ.

Blessing many for the sake of the godly few

When God was about to destroy Sodom, Abraham pleaded with Him to spare the whole city if fifty righteous people lived there. The Lord graciously replied, 'If I find in Sodom fifty righteous within the city, then I will spare the whole place on their account' (Genesis 18:26). Picking up on that graciousness, the compassionate patriarch further interceded with the Lord, asking if He would reduce the number to forty-five, then forty, then thirty, then twenty, and finally ten. In each case the Lord mercifully agreed to spare the city, but not even ten righteous people could be found therein. Nevertheless, it stands for us for all time that God was willing to bless many wicked people for the sake of just a few of His own people in their midst.

God looks on the family as a unit. Even if it is divided spiritually and most of its members are unbelieving and immoral, the entire family is graced by the presence of a believer. Therefore, if an unbelieving spouse is willing to stay, the believer is not to seek a divorce.

Christians need not fear that their children will be unclean, defiled by the unbelieving father or mother. God promises that the opposite is true: 'otherwise your children are unclean, but now they are holy' (verse 14). They would be unclean if both parents were unbelievers, but the Lord guarantees that the presence of just one Christian parent will protect the children. It is not that their salvation is assured, but that they are protected from undue spiritual harm, and they will receive spiritual blessings. 'They are holy' in the sense that they share in the spiritual benefits of their believing parent. Often the testimony of the believing parent is especially effective in this situation because the children see a clear contrast to the unbelieving parent's life, and that leads them to see their own need for salvation.

Guidelines for Christians married to unbelievers who want to leave

An entirely different situation is when an unbeliever resents his or her spouse's faith in Christ and wants to leave the marriage. God's Word, therefore, gives different instructions from those for the previous scenario: 'Yet if the unbelieving one leaves, let him leave; the brother or the sister is not under bondage in such cases, but God has called us to peace. For how do you know, O wife, whether you will save your husband? Or how do you know, O husband, whether you will save your wife?' (1 Corinthians 7:15–16). The church father Tertullian, when discussing this text, gave the example of pagan husbands who were furious that their Christian wives would visit the cottages of the poor, alleviate martyrs' bonds, and treat fellow Christians as brothers and sisters. Many non-believing husbands today feel such revulsion for Christian love and ministry that their sin compels them to move in the opposite direction, leaving their Christian wives behind.

Paul's word from the Lord is that any Christian wife or husband in that situation is not to try to insist that the unbelieving spouse stay if he or she is determined to go. 'If the unbelieving one leaves, let him leave.' The Greek word translated 'leave' (*chorizo*) is a specific reference to divorce. If the unbeliever begins divorce proceedings, the Christian is not to contest them. 'The brother or the sister is not under bondage in such cases' (verse 15). In God's sight, the bond between a husband and wife is dissolved only by death (Romans 7:2), adultery (Matthew 19:9), and an unbeliever's leaving (1 Corinthians 7:15). When the bond is broken in any of those ways, a Christian is free to remarry another Christian or stay single. Simply stated, when divorce is permitted, remarriage is permitted; when divorce is forbidden, remarriage is forbidden.

God has called us to peace

God allows divorce when a non-Christian deserts his or her Christian spouse because He 'has called us to peace' (verse 15). If the unbelieving husband or wife cannot tolerate the spouse's faith in Christ and desires to be free from the union, it is better that the marriage be dissolved to preserve the peace of His child. Constant fighting, turmoil, criticism, and frustration over the spouse's faith will disrupt the harmony and peace that God wants His children to have in their faith. God hates divorce, but He hates the undermining of His children's faith in His Son even more. Jesus said, 'Whoever causes one of these little ones who believe in Me to stumble, it would be better for him to have a heavy millstone hung around his neck, and to be drowned in the depth of the sea' (Matthew 18:6). Letting the adamant unbelieving spouse depart is a merciful concession by God, sparing the unbeliever stricter judgment and the believer unnecessary temptation. If that unbeliever is not concerned with a legal divorce and simply abandons the believing spouse, the believer is free to apply for divorce after a reasonable period of time. God's Word declares that the brother or sister in Christ 'is not under bondage in such cases' (1 Corinthians 7:15). Desertion is like adultery in that it disrupts the marital tie or bond.

That is an extreme situation, however, and most Christians will not find themselves in it. The opposite extreme is when a believer with an unbelieving spouse sees someone who seems better, so the believer deliberately tries to make life difficult for the unbeliever, hoping to provoke that person to bail out of the marriage. Those who deliberately abuse scriptural technicalities for ungodly purposes will reap what they have sowed. God looks at the heart and knows the truth of every situation. He knows whether the unbelieving spouse really abandoned the marriage, and He knows whether the believing partner truly sought to be a sanctifying influence in hopes of winning the unbelieving spouse to saving faith in Jesus Christ. Those who deliberately drive their spouses away dishonor and displease the Lord.

'If possible,' says Paul in Romans 12:18, 'so far as it depends on you, be at peace with all men.' That is not always possible, especially in a marriage with a non-Christian, but most times it is when we are patient, kind, considerate, humble, and flexible. That is why we read in 1 Peter 3:1–2, 'You wives, be submissive to your own husbands so that even if any of them are disobedient to the word, they may be won without a word by the behavior of their wives, as they observe your chaste and respectful behavior.' But when an unbeliever wants out of a marriage, the peace no longer depends on the Christian. Many Christians have tried to keep a marriage together even when the spouse was unbelieving and wanted a divorce. Sometimes they have even compromised their Christian principles in a desperate bid to prevent the divorce. That is against God's will: 'Let him leave' (1 Corinthians 7:15) is a command, not a mere statement granting permission.

Verse 16 explains that a wife has no assurance that she will save her husband, and a husband has no assurance that he will save his wife. It is God, of course, who does the saving of anyone's soul. Verse 16 is worded the way it is to keep the Christian husband or wife from *assuming* that God will use him or her to lead the non-believing spouse to saving faith in Christ. Regardless of the Christian's best motives and hopes, if the unbelieving partner stays married to that Christian unwillingly or reluctantly, the likelihood of that partner's turning to Christ is small, and the disruption of family peace is assured. The Lord therefore allows no option.

Evangelism is not cause enough to maintain a marriage when the unbelieving partner wants to leave. The believer is to entrust that spouse's soul to God, trusting Him to use whomever He will to take up the call to repentance and faith in Christ.

A summary of biblical options for single and married people

If you are single, you fall into one of four categories. Category one is what I call *Single by Delay*. You're single but you're not going to stay that way. This is just a delay until you can get married to the person God is preparing for you. What does the Word say to you? Get married, 'for it is better to marry than to burn with passion' (verse 9). Be both patient and proactive.

You are in category two if you are *Single by Divine Design* for unhindered service to Christ. What should you do? Stay single and minister with all your heart, full of joy. What if you are *Single by Divorce*, category three? Seriously consider first whether you have been gifted by God to be single for such blessed service. If you were divorced out of an adulterous situation, if your divorce was before you were saved, or if an unbeliever divorced you, you are free to marry a Christian. The fourth category of singleness is if you are *Single by Death*. Stay single if you are so gifted, but if you are not, get married to a believer.

What about married people? If you are married to either a Christian or a non-Christian, stay married and enjoy the blessings of obedience. Hard-hearted, unrepentant adultery is the only legitimate basis for divorce that Jesus gave. Also, in the extreme situation where a non-Christian spouse wants nothing to do with you because of your faith in Christ, let him or her depart. God does not hold you bound to such a union.

As you can see, the Bible is clear on the topics of marriage, singleness, divorce, and remarriage. Will you obey what it teaches for God's sake and your own? Whatever God has given you as your marital state, accept it as His will, and maximize it for His glory.

What about those who opted out of the biblical options?

What if you got a divorce as a Christian, but not for one of the two legitimate reasons? What if you then remarried and tainted yourself and your new spouse with the sin of adultery? What is your status? You are a sinner. Confess your sin, tell God the sorrow of your heart, and stay in the marriage you now are in. See if God will not make sweet out of the bitter. Another divorce at this point would compound the sin, rather than undoing the sin of the first divorce. That is a sin that cannot be undone at this point. Returning to the first spouse after a second marriage would be an abomination in God's eyes according to Deuteronomy 24:1–4.

The truth is that 'we all stumble in many ways' (James 3:2). There is good news, however: 'If we confess our sins, He is faithful and righteous to forgive us our sins and to cleanse us from all unrighteousness' (1 John 1:9). God has mercy on those who are humble and of a contrite heart. With such men and women in mind, Jesus said, 'Any sin and blasphemy shall be forgiven people' (Matthew 12:31). In a very real sense, Jesus is in the sin-forgiving business. Thank God for the grace that you are still alive and make the most out of the union you have. Earnestly seek never to tread on His grace again.

Going on the high road with God

This concludes our careful study of the three key texts in Matthew 5, Matthew 19, and 1 Corinthians 7 that directly speak about divorce, remarriage, and God's ideal for marriage. They challenge us to take the high road with the Lord, not the low road with the world around us.

God indeed calls us to peace—with Him and with one another—in our lives and marriages through our faith in the Lord Jesus Christ and the power of His indwelling Holy Spirit. The Christian classic *Hinds' Feet on High Places* explains in its Preface that the High Places of victory and union with Christ come 'by a continually repeated laying down of our own will and acceptance of His as it is presented to us *in the form of the people with whom we have to live* and work, and in the things which happen to us. Every acceptance of His will becomes an altar of sacrifice, and every such surrender and abandonment of ourselves to His will is a means of furthering us on the way to the High Places to which He desires to bring every child of His while they are still living on earth.'

Another Christian classic, *The Imitation of Christ*, offers up this prayer on 'How One Should Feel and Speak on Every Desirable Thing,' including marriage: 'Grant what You will, as much as You will, when You will. Do with me as You know best, as will most please You, and will be for Your greater honor.' Amen.

8   Questions and answers

Here are some questions on marriage, divorce, and remarriage that I have been asked to answer through the years. Bear in mind that I am very far from infallible—as my family can affirm! My replies are right only insofar as I have based them on biblical truth and rightly applied it. I hope they will encourage you and provide guidance to help you know and do the will of God.

Q1. If you are a believer married to a non-Christian man who brings a divorce action, then repents, and comes back to you to ask to resume the relationship and get married again, what should you do? You have not remarried. Should you begin to see him again, and maybe get married again?

A1. If he is still not a believer in Christ, the Scriptures forbid you to marry him (1 Corinthians 7:39; 9:5). If the mentioned repentance helped him to see his need for a Savior from his sin and embrace Jesus Christ in faith since 'there is no other name under heaven … by which we must be saved' (Acts 4:12), then remarrying him is a possibility. I do not recommend that course of action, however, because his faith is genuine only if it rests entirely in Christ. He chose to separate himself from you, and God released you from your tie to him (1 Corinthians 7:15). He needs to resist the temptation to cling to you now, as if you will automatically become a reward for his faith. Encourage him to trust in Christ to meet all his needs, and be spiritually trained (discipled) by a pastor or other Christian leader. Let him know you have fully forgiven him of all the past (be sure you mean it from the heart), but that you think it is best for you both to remain as friends. How he responds will be a telling indicator of his heart, thus giving you further guidance.

Q2. Adultery is not the only possible painful ingredient in a marriage. What do you recommend when there is child molestation, pornography, violence, extreme alcoholism, and other situations that pass beyond being marginal into what seems intolerable for the other spouse?

A2. When our Lord on the cross was suffering the full fury of divine wrath for the sins of the whole world, He cried out, 'My God, My God, why have You forsaken Me?' (Matthew 27:46). Among the darkest of all those sins upon which the Father turned His back are the ones perpetrated against helpless women and children. Know first that Jesus understands and has done something significant about the source of your grief. In the case of child molestation, which is a form of adultery, He has provided a way out for you by permitting divorce and remarriage (Matthew 5:32; 19:8–9). The same is true in the case of pornography if, as is often true, it has led to adulterous behavior. If it has not, the believing spouse needs to confront the sinning spouse in love, pointing out that Jesus said, 'Everyone who looks at a woman with lust for her has already committed adultery with her in his heart' (Matthew 5:28). The Word of God is to be brought to bear regarding violence, alcohol abuse, and whatever else is troubling the marriage, and the sinning partner held accountable not only by the faithful spouse, but also by a godly pastor, family members, and even civil authorities in cases where the laws of the land are being violated. Seek shelter from God's people when needed, but do not seek to end a marriage that God has given you no right to end. Your Heavenly Father is watching over you, and will richly reward you for honoring your vow to love your spouse 'for better or worse'—two aspects that are present in every marriage.

Q3. If the church where an adulterously guilty man and his wife are members is evangelical, but has a flawed view of the biblical approach to marriage, divorce, and remarriage and has a very weak approach to church discipline, how should I seek to help the spouses concerned, who are my friends? I go to another church.

A3. You are right to bring up the topic of church discipline, but don't think you need to have a perfect church to begin applying Matthew 18:15–20, the key text on handling sin with discipline and prayer. Jesus said,

If your brother sins, go and show him his fault in private; if he listens to you, you have won your brother. But if he does not listen to you, take one or two more with you, so that by the mouth of two or three witnesses every fact may be confirmed. If he refuses to listen to them, tell it to the church; and if he refuses to listen even to the church, let him be to you as a Gentile and a tax collector ... Where two or three have gathered together in My name [to encourage a sinning brother or sister to repent], I am there in their midst.

You need to talk to your adulterous friend privately, letting him know what you know. Ask him if he has confessed the truth to his wife, for he has sinned against her. Urge him to confess and repent before God, his wife, and his partner in adultery. If he has been maintaining a façade at his church, share with him these words from Jesus: 'If you are presenting your offering at the altar, and there remember that your brother [or sister] has something against you, leave your offering there before the altar and go; first be reconciled to your brother, and then come and present your offering' (Matthew 5:23–24). If your friend will not listen to you, confide in one or two trustworthy men from his church, and arrange to meet together with your friend over an open Bible. If he still won't repent, the two or three of you need to meet with the pastor of the church. If he doesn't listen even to the pastor, then at least the façade is gone, and you and his church know to regard him as an unbeliever (and his wife worthy of extra support and compassion). As you would want to do with any other unbeliever, help him recognize his dire need for forgiveness of his sins to escape eternal damnation by submitting himself to Christ as Savior and Lord. Know that Christ Himself will be backing you up every step of the way.

Q4. My friend has all the biblical reasons to allow remarriage, but she feels that she made her marriage vow not only to her husband, but to God. Even though he has broken his vow, she feels she remains bound to her vow to God and that, therefore, she cannot remarry while her husband is still living. Please would you comment?

A4. I would begin with 1 Corinthians 7, commending her for understanding and applying two of Paul's main themes: that it can be good for her as an unmarried woman to remain single, and that it is best for her to be content with her current marital status, not quick to change it. Then I would ask her to read verse 15: 'If the unbelieving one leaves, let him leave; the brother or the sister is not under bondage in such cases,' asking her, 'Since God does not consider a woman in that situation to be bound to her marriage vows anymore, would it be right for the woman to consider herself still bound?' My hope is that she will see that no one has a higher regard for what is right than God does. Then I would apply the same reasoning toward the exception clauses regarding adultery in Matthew 5:32 and Matthew 19:9. I would go back to 1 Corinthians 7 and encourage her to consider before God whether she has been specially gifted with singleness (verses 7–8) or not (verse 9). May her gifting, not false guilt, be her guide.

Q5. If a marriage has been broken up by a third party, how can the innocent party have the right Christian attitude towards that third party who caused the divorce? How does that person fight against bitterness and resentment? How does he or she deal with the guilt produced by that?

A5. Those are noble questions, reflecting the heart of a mature believer ready to obey Ephesians 4:32: 'Be kind to one another, tender-hearted, forgiving each other, just as God in Christ also has forgiven you.' When I think—really think hard—about all Christ has forgiven me for, it makes it easier for me to forgive others who have hurt me. Then I think about what Christ wants to accomplish in those people's lives, asking Him if He will give me the privilege of representing Him well to those people as a way of drawing them to Him. Remember, we

formerly lived in the lusts of our flesh, indulging the desires of the flesh and of the mind, and were by nature children of wrath, even as the rest. But God, being rich in mercy, because of His great love with which He loved us, even when we were dead in our transgressions, made us alive together with Christ ... and raised us up with Him, and seated us with Him in the heavenly places in Christ Jesus, so that in the ages to come He might show the surpassing riches of His grace in kindness toward us in Christ Jesus (Ephesians 2:3–7).

When you think about God's love for you that way, you will find yourself having compassion for those who are missing out because of sins they are clinging to.

Q6. There is a lot of divorce and remarriage within many Christian churches. Should divorced people be remarried within the church building or fellowship without any church discipline being imposed?

A6. When I was a new pastor, I was asked to perform the wedding ceremony for two people who had no biblical right to be joined together. When I said no, it was suggested that someone else could do the ceremony. I responded that the ceremony should not take place at our church if our church was indeed Christ's church, and the elders agreed. Jesus said, 'If you love Me, you will keep My commandments' (John 14:15). The church that loves Jesus Christ will have in its midst only those weddings that are in accord with His Word. It will not bow to pressure, and then seek to discipline or ask God's forgiveness afterwards.

Q7. How should the members of a family deal with a parent who is a Christian but has gone through with a divorce, or is just about to? How should the children relate to that parent? How do you balance honoring your parents in this situation, especially if one of them is under church discipline, or should be?

A7. In Matthew 18:15–20, the church-discipline text I referred to under Question 3, of the people who are trying to woo the sinning brother to repent, godly family members have a key role to play from first to last. Read that text carefully and what I wrote about it. Be there with your mom and dad and that open Bible, pleading for him or her to obey what he or she once taught you about being a faithful husband or wife. If your parent keeps refusing, let him or her know you will be obliged to regard him or her as an unbeliever, whom you will continue to love and pray for, but from whom you fear you will be separated for eternity unless he or she repents. Maybe, once upon a time, your parent said something similar to you when you were going through a period of rebellion. Keep promoting repentance, and should that joyfully occur, encourage a complete reconciliation if both of your parents are still unmarried. If one or both have remarried, they can still fully and freely forgive each other, and seek to honor God in the marriages they are now in. Continue to honor your parents, which by extension includes any other spouses, and leave the sins of the past in the past so they can do no more damage.

Q8. If soon after a marriage, one party finds the other was immoral just before the marriage, how do both parties deal with that?

A8. Repentance and forgiveness need to take place, but how forthcoming that will be depends on how you found out about the immorality. Did your partner openly and humbly confess to you? If so, your mate is displaying a heart that is tender toward the working of God's Spirit, who would not want him to worship or do anything else until he is right with you. That is the spirit of the Matthew 5:23–24 text I cited earlier: When a man realizes his wife has something against him (whether she realizes it or not beforehand), God wants him first to be reconciled to his wife. If that is what your spouse is trying to do, be gracious for God's sake as well as for his, and that can form a great foundation of trust for your future years together. If, however, you had to find out about your spouse's immorality the hard way, that will understandably be harder on your emotions. Keep a biblical illustration in mind: When King David did something far worse than your spouse by committing adultery with Bathsheba and arranging for the murder of her spouse, he did not confess his sins at first, but went through an elaborate series of cover-ups. He confessed only when directly confronted by the prophet Nathan and warned about judgment related to his sins. David then 'said to Nathan, "I have sinned against the LORD." And Nathan said to David, "The LORD also has taken away your sin; you shall not die"' (2 Samuel 12:13). David did suffer consequences from his sin, just as you and your spouse may suffer consequences from the pre-marital immorality (medical or otherwise), but David admitted his sin and was forgiven. God was gracious to David and Bathsheba. They later had Solomon, at whose birth the Lord sent word for him to be nicknamed Jedidiah, which means 'beloved of the LORD.' If your spouse says, 'I have sinned against the Lord,' forgive him or her just as the Lord forgave David, who wrote of this experience in Psalm 51. His prayer can be your own: 'Restore to me the joy of Your salvation and sustain me with a willing spirit. Then I will teach transgressors Your ways, and sinners will be converted to You' (verses 12–13). If you allow it to, your situation can work out for great good in the conviction with which you and your spouse teach any future children and others about God's standards for holiness and purity.

Q9. In Deuteronomy 24:1–4, since the woman was divorced for a lesser reason than adultery and then remarried, is it not true that her second marriage was not a marriage at all, but just an adulterous situation? Since the second marriage ended, why couldn't there be a remarriage between the first partners? Isn't it God's ideal to keep a true marriage together?

A9. Yes, it is God's ideal to keep a true marriage together, but in the case of Deuteronomy 24, the husband who effectively sent his wife into the arms of another man violated his marriage vow and created an adulterous situation. That sin would need to be dealt with before any restoration could be possible, and no provision for the sin is named in Deuteronomy 24. It is assumed that the sin still remained, and it could not be ignored because of God's holiness, so that is why the man was forbidden to take back his former wife if he happened to feel like it and the opportunity presented itself with the dissolving of his wife's second marriage. Yet now, because of what Christ accomplished on the cross for all who embrace it by faith, He has 'forgiven us all our transgressions, having canceled out the certificate of debt consisting of decrees against us, which was hostile to us; and *He has taken it out of the way*, having nailed it to the cross' (Colossians 2:13–14, emphasis added). That includes past marital sins. If a man and woman who were originally married have the opportunity to come together again as husband and wife, they may do so with God's approval if they both have repented of their sins and trusted in Christ as their Savior and Lord.

Q10. How should a Christian wife deal with an unfaithful husband who wants to keep his wife for security, reputation, and a place to stay? If she needs to let him go, how does she know when she has reached that point?

A10. She needs to sit down with him and lovingly but firmly present him with some biblical realities about marriage. First, I suggest that she asks him to read Matthew 5:31–32 out loud and ask him what Jesus declared in the Sermon on the Mount to be the only exception for something as dreadful as divorce. Then she should ask him to read Matthew 19:3–9, pointing out the same exception, and ask him if he is willing from this point on to cease violating her one-flesh union with him, for that is the only way he can avoid being in the truly terrible position of separating what God has joined together. While it is true she is not required to divorce him for his adulteries, that should not enter into the discussion at this point since he has been abusing God's grace and his wife's graciousness. Since 'the fear of the LORD is the beginning of wisdom, and the knowledge of the Holy One is understanding' (Proverbs 9:10), square one is to help him realize the peril of his soul by violating what he is now facing in God's Word. Hold up God's high standard for marriage so he knows what God will help him aim for if he will but ask. Read Ephesians 5:25–31 together:

Husbands, love your wives, just as Christ also loved the church and gave Himself up for her, so that He might sanctify her, having cleansed her by the washing of water with the word, that He might present to Himself the church in all her glory, having no spot or wrinkle or any such thing; but that she would be holy and blameless. So husbands ought also to love their own wives as their own bodies. He who loves his own wife loves himself; for no one ever hated his own flesh, but nourishes and cherishes it, just as Christ also does the church, because we are members of His body. For this reason a man shall leave his father and mother and shall be joined to his wife, and the two shall become one flesh.

It goes back to the one-flesh union: Will the adulterous husband preserve it, trusting in God and mature Christians to help him, or not? For the wife, can she tolerate it being broken anymore, or not? Only she can answer that question.

Q11. Does the Bible say anything about separation that falls short of divorce? Is it allowed? If so, on what grounds is it allowed? Is it correct that the 1 Corinthians 7 basis for divorce requires no legal action from the abandoning party? If he or she just disappears, is that sufficient reason for the Christian spouse to seek a divorce? If not, what should the abandoned party do to prove that he or she has been forsaken?

A11. The only voluntary marital separation permitted in Scripture is detailed in 1 Corinthians 7:4–5:

The wife does not have authority over her own body, but the husband does; and likewise also the husband does not have authority over his own body, but the wife does. Stop depriving one another, except by agreement for a time, so that you may devote yourselves to prayer, and come together again so that Satan will not tempt you because of your lack of self-control.

It is to be by mutual agreement, temporary, and for a spiritual purpose. Separating after an argument is the sinful first step toward abandonment, which is the first step toward divorce. Separation leads to sexual temptation, which the enemy of our souls would love to use to tempt aggrieved spouses into adultery, for that is how he would attempt to destroy God's work in a marriage. Do not give him that opportunity. Work out your marriage problems together, in person, for God is in your midst to keep together what He has joined together, but you need to trust Him together. Stubborn abandonment indicates the lack of true saving faith in Christ, for 1 Corinthians 7:15 states, 'If the unbelieving one leaves, let him leave; the brother or the sister is not under bondage in such cases, but God has called us to peace.' The Apostle John, writing about people who seemed like Christians but left the fellowship of genuine believers, declared, 'They went out from us, but they were not really of us; for if they had been of us, they would have remained with us; but they went out, so that it would be shown that they ... are not of us' (1 John 2:19). Therefore, God gives the Christian husband or wife who has been so abandoned freedom from the bond of that union, either by filing for divorce according to the laws of the land regarding the length of abandonment, or by submitting to the divorce served by the abandoning partner. Do all you can to put the fear of God into that spouse, however, challenging him or her that an eternal destiny is at stake.

Q12. Why do some teach that if a marriage has been ended by divorce because of adultery or because a non-Christian spouse would not remain with his or her Christian partner, only the innocent party is free to remarry? Is that not an emotional rather than a biblical argument?

A12. No, it is not, because this is our main message to the non-Christian (or anyone acting like one): 'God is now declaring to men that all people everywhere should repent, because He has fixed a day in which He will judge the world in righteousness through a Man whom He has appointed, having furnished proof to all men by raising Him from the dead' (Acts 17:30–31). The same man who uttered those words wrote, 'What have

I to do with judging outsiders? Do you not judge those who are within the church? But those who are outside, God judges. Remove the wicked man from among yourselves' (1 Corinthians 5:12–13). Some Christians, admiring the boldness of John the Baptist in confronting King Herod's adultery (Matthew 14:3–4), get the wrong idea that they are to preach moral reform to non-Christians, even if it is apart from saving faith in the Redeemer. Jesus warned of the danger of reformation without regeneration by giving this illustration:

When the unclean spirit goes out of a man, it passes through waterless places seeking rest, and does not find it. Then it says, 'I will return to my house from which I came'; and when it comes, it finds it unoccupied, swept, and put in order. Then it goes and takes along with it seven other spirits more wicked than itself, and they go in and live there; and the last state of that man becomes worse than the first (Matthew 12:43–45).

That is to become like a Pharisee, smug in what he thinks he can get away with regarding marriage or other matters—like those who 'rejected God's purpose for themselves, not having been baptized by John' (Luke 7:30). Herod used to meet with John, and although Scripture does not record exactly what they talked about, we can be sure that he who preached 'a baptism of repentance for the forgiveness of sins' (Mark 1:4) emphasized Herod's need for repentance. The subject of Herod's marriage obviously came up as one of what were certainly many illustrations of that need. We do know what Paul, in similar circumstances, talked about to the governor Felix: 'righteousness, self-control and the judgment to come' (Acts 24:25). Paul was helping the governor to understand his need for a Savior. That is what you and I need to emphasize when talking to non-Christians, regardless of their marital or other personal problems. They need first to repent and submit to Christ as Savior and Lord. Only then do we move on to, as Jesus said, 'teaching them to observe all that I commanded you' (Matthew 28:20).

Q13. Matthew 5:32 and 19:9 use the terms 'unchastity,' 'immorality,' and 'adultery' as legitimate grounds for divorce. In discreet yet clear terms, what kind of behavior is being referred to? Does this have any application to sexual behavior within the marriage?

A13. The Greek word translated 'unchastity' or 'immorality' (*porneia*) refers to any illicit sexual intercourse, whether either of the parties is married or not. It is a broad term that includes adultery. *Porneia* also includes incest (involving blood relatives, legal relatives, or children), prostitution, homosexuality, and bestiality. Here is how this applies to marriage, in the discreet yet clear terms of Scripture:

Drink water from your own cistern
And fresh water from your own well.
Should your springs be dispersed abroad,
Streams of water in the streets?
Let them be yours alone
And not for strangers with you.
Let your fountain be blessed,
And rejoice in the wife of your youth.
As a loving hind and a graceful doe,
Let her breasts satisfy you at all times;
Be exhilarated always with her love.
For why should you, my son, be exhilarated with an adulteress
And embrace the bosom of a foreigner?
For the ways of a man are before the eyes of the LORD,
And He watches all his paths (Proverbs 5:15–21).

Your private parts are to be reserved for your marital partner's pleasure, not for anyone else's. That is how to keep 'the marriage bed ... undefiled' (Hebrews 13:4). The exhilaration that comes from your love is a private matter of mutual agreement between you and your spouse. God is watching over your marriage, and 'fornicators and adulterers God will judge' (Hebrews 13:4), so keep private what He wants you to keep private.

Q14. What practical advice would you give to a married couple who have no experience of using their home for Christ, but now want to?

A14. This is a great ministry, because many young Christians, and some older ones, have never seen any marriage work before their eyes. Open your home to provide a wide variety of hospitality. Let it become a sympathetic oasis in a troubled world where people can talk over their problems and joys in the light of God's Word. By holding informal meetings and Bible studies in a non-threatening home atmosphere, you will see people come to Christ who would never have stepped into a church first. Your home can also become a place to encourage visiting missionaries, to relieve stressed pastors and their wives, to provide refuge for battered wives or forsaken spouses and their children, and to invite single friends for a refreshing home ambiance and enjoyable exposure to family life.

Q15. How can Christian family members help when their Christian children are having serious marriage problems?

A15. Be available to pray and give biblical counsel. Do not give up. Godly family members can be greatly used by God to help the innocent and guilty parties respond the way He wants them to.

Appendix: 'Dear Joe ...' A father shares his broken heart

Here is a powerful example to encourage you to do all you can to help save that marriage. It is a letter from the father of a young wife to her unfaithful husband. All names and some details have been changed to hide true identities and situations. It is reproduced now with the gracious consent of the man who wrote it. Repentance and reconciliation followed later, and the husband concerned is now working out his renewed relationship with his wife!

Dear Joe,

You promised me that you would meet with me, yet you have not responded to the alternative dates I sent you. You have made no attempt to contact me. It is time we met. I have heard that you say you are scared to meet with me. Why? You don't work for me, so I cannot fire you. I am not a judge, so I cannot impose any penalty on you. You know I would not assault you, and in any case you are much younger, bigger, and stronger than I am. Why then are you scared?

I think you fear I may trouble your conscience. It is said that conscience makes cowards of us all. If I am right, Joe, you are treading very dangerously. You are like the man who was so worried about the connection between smoking and lung cancer that he gave up reading! Are you concerned about your sin, or are you only concerned about the unease you feel when you are reminded of it? When our consciences work to challenge our wrong behavior, it is utmost folly to try to silence them.

Your seeming reluctance to meet with me encourages me in one way, however. If your conscience needs such diligent protection, it must still be functioning to some degree. If that is so, you have not yet reached the condition of the apostate people whose consciences had become so hardened and unable to respond to guilt, Paul wrote that they were 'seared as with a hot iron' (1 Timothy 4:2).

Although a letter lacks many advantages of a one-to-one dialogue, it gives me the chance to ask you how you will respond to questions I will put to you if and when we do meet. I did remind you at our last meeting of God's mercy and grace as He deals with us in forgiveness and restoration, even after the most serious sin, if we come to Him by turning from that sin in repentance and seeking His forgiveness. That is still so.

We looked together at 1 John 1:6–9, where we are told to 'walk in the Light,' and I urged on you the need for openness and honesty with God (who knows anyhow), with Lisa, who desperately needs reassurance, and with others.

I know you met with Pastor Harry. I do not know what he said, but I am sure he would have endorsed what I said to you. He has put in so much time on this. With his wife he has been counseling Lisa. She has tried to act on their advice. Your parents, along with Lisa's mom and me, are praying our socks off for you! We will do anything to help because we love Lisa, your two kids, and you, Joe. But what have you done about putting yourself and the situation right?

What happened to that openness and honesty we discussed? Have you repented of your moral infidelity and all those lies? Do you accept personal responsibility and blame? Your letter to me said 'after what has happened …' as if it were a disease, accident, or crime over which you had no control. But we are dealing with what you chose to do. It did not 'happen.' You are directly responsible and culpable. Nothing will ever be achieved until you stop evading responsibility. In Psalm 51 David had to tell God, 'I acknowledge my transgressions, and my sin is ever before me' and 'I have sinned and done evil in Your sight.' Do you feel your guilt, Joe? If so, how are you dealing with that guilt?

Let me deal with what love really is. Why does God command husbands to love their wives, even though we know that people fall in love and seemingly fall out of love, too? If love is beyond our control, it seems unfair of God to command us to do something we have no control over. Is God teasing us? Of course not! The confusion comes from two different concepts signified by the same English word, love.

Those words in the Greek language of the New Testament are *eros* and *agapē*. Pastor John MacArthur describes *eros* as the love that takes. A person with *eros* loves someone for what he can get from that person. Perhaps there may be incidental giving, too, but the driver is the pursuit of personal pleasure. It is the love that typifies the world, self-gratifying and lustful. Although it includes sexual desire, there is more to it than that, and sometimes the object of that kind of love becomes an idol in a spiritual sense.

Another characteristic of *eros* is unreliability. We can fall in and out of this kind of love. It offers no security and is mainly immediate and sensual. Most of us experience it at some time in our lives, and most marriages start with a large dose of it. But truly secure marriages are not built on *eros* alone. If marriages are made in heaven, the best marriages are characterized by the love that comes from heaven.

Eros is not the 'Husbands, love your wives' type of love. That love is *agapē* love. *Agapē* is the same love (in kind but obviously not in quality) that Christ has for His bride, the church. It gives. It does not take. It seeks others' highest good, no matter what the cost. It is completely unselfish. This is God's love for the world in John 3:16. Jesus said, 'Greater love has no man than this, that a man lays down his life for his friend' (John 15:13). That, too, is *agapē*.

The world exalts *eros*. This self-gratifying emotion epitomizes the spirit of the present age. The arts and media depict it as an all-conquering power to which we must submit. They say it is futile to fight against such feelings because they constitute inevitable progress toward our destiny. We are taught that 'All We Need Is Love' (meaning *eros*), as if this unreliable, self-gratifying emotion is the very purpose of our existence. Those resisting its allurements are caricatured as outdated Puritans who understand nothing about matters of the heart. Such is the underlying consensus of the godless society in which we live. Such are the lies that Satan plants in the hearts of sinful, rebellious people.

But the Bible exalts *agapē* love. First Corinthians 13 gives a full description of it: *Agapē* is patient, kind, not jealous, not boastful, not arrogant, not unbecoming, not self-seeking, not easily angered, not keeping a record of wrongs, not happy about unrighteousness, but happy in the truth, and willing to bear all things, believe all things, hope all things, and endure all things. There is often a conflict between *eros* and *agapē*. Have you ever been aware of that conflict yourself, Joe?

Would you say that you have demonstrated *agapē* love over the last year and a half for Lisa, for your kids, or for Janet, the woman you chose instead of your wife? Let me look at each case.

Do you know what emotional anguish and suffering you have caused Lisa because of your sin? Do you care? When you asked me if you could marry her, I told you that I was about to trust you with the most precious thing a man can ever entrust to another: his daughter. I remember impressing on you your responsibility as a husband to care for your wife not only materially, but also emotionally and spiritually. You have also let me down, Joe. Are you going to continue to let me down?

How about Mark and Grace? Do you know that those two lovely little children have a fundamental need of a mother who is secure in her husband's love? That is a far greater need than for a daddy who has weekly contact to try to salve his own conscience. Have you been showing them real *agapē* love over the last eighteen months? Will you show them real *agapē* love in the future? Research has shown clearly that children from broken homes are more likely to suffer from emotional problems, and less likely to succeed academically than those brought up with both parents in a stable home. I myself have seen over many years the distress, insecurity, and learning difficulties caused by marital breakup. I am appalled to think you intend to inflict such a future on Mark and Grace.

If Grace found herself in the same position in a few years' time, how would you feel as a father? Would you do all you could to help her rebuild her marriage? Would you spend time praying for her, her wayward husband, and her kids? Would you find yourself thinking about her emotional and spiritual needs, day and night? Would you? If not, then you would not feel as I feel. If your feelings would be like mine, then why not start showing that kind of love for your daughter, and for your son, right now?

I turn to Janet. Do you know how you have damaged her by your immoral behavior? Do not tell me, 'There was nothing we could do about it.' We can always choose *agapē* instead of *eros*, and God will help us as we do. Like a demon god, *eros* may demand the sacrifice of your wife, your children, your integrity, and your faith. The force of *eros* is so strong that, for many, conformity to its demands seems almost inevitable. This is hardly surprising when we remember that Satan is the prince of this world. What hope do we have to resist such a powerful voice? None within ourselves, but in Christ we have all the resources of God at our disposal, if we have repentant hearts and sincerely desire to walk in His ways.

Self-giving love is not a compulsive obsession with another person. On the contrary, that kind of selfless love is a willingness never to see them again, if that is for their greater and ultimate good. The best thing you can do for

Janet is to ask her forgiveness, pray that God will overrule all the damage you have done, and then get out of her life finally and completely. Make the break.

When we meet I want to know what your plans are for the future. Lisa has suffered appalling humiliation. I want to hear from your own mouth what your intentions are for your wife, your children, and your mistress. Will you continue to manipulate and take advantage of Lisa, and to rob Mark and Grace of a mother who is secure in the love of her husband? Will your determination to gratify your own desires cause the continuation of your willful cruelty toward your children and my daughter? Are you going to continue to pursue your own 'happiness' regardless of the pain you inflict on others? Will you carry on valuing money and position more than decency and honor?

We are still at square one. I repeat the questions I asked you at our last meeting, all that time ago. How will you assure Lisa of your love and care for her materially, emotionally, and spiritually? How will you regain her trust? How will you fulfill your responsibility toward Lisa and the children? Do you imagine you can do any of that without first getting right with God? Have you spent time in crying out to Him for mercy, strength, wisdom, and help since we last met? Have you prayed for yourself, as David did in Psalm 51? Have you prayed for all those you have hurt—Lisa, Mark, Grace, and Janet—as we have, along with your parents? Will you plead with God, as I do, to heal the hurt your sin has inflicted upon them, and will continue to inflict on them, unless you really repent and come back to God? I urge you to pray for a repentant heart, first of all, and then for Lisa and the kids, that they will make a good recovery from the damage you have caused.

I look forward to meeting you and hearing your responses to those questions. Satan will tell you to avoid that meeting to protect your conscience from guilt for a little longer. He is striving for it to become 'seared' and insensitive. He will, therefore, continue to encourage your thinking that you have no control over your actions, and that thus you are without responsibility. He lies. You are responsible!

When we meet, I challenge you to stop excusing yourself, pretending to be a passive victim of circumstance, and to have the courage to accept responsibility for your own actions. If you wonder why repentance is hard to come by, it is because you must first acknowledge the sinfulness of your sin.

If you have decided to desert your wife and children to continue your adulterous affair, then when we meet you must acknowledge your responsibility for that decision. You must say to my face the following words: 'Martin, I repudiate the agreement I made with you to love and care for your daughter. I also renounce my marriage vows made before many witnesses and disaffirm my Christian profession. I reject God, my wife, and my children and explicitly refuse to fulfill my responsibilities toward them.'

Awful though such a declaration would be, it would be more honest than pretending that things 'happen' over which you have no control. On the other hand, if God works through your afflicted conscience to create within your heart a sense of responsibility for your sin, and a godly sorrow that leads to repentance (2 Corinthians 7:10), I would love to pray with you. I would value the opportunity to ask God's blessing on your life and to encourage you to exercise saving faith in the Lord Jesus, whose blood is able to save us from all sin. I would also like to discuss any ways in which I might be able to help you in the future.

The contents of this letter are no more confidential than you wish to make them. I am sending a copy to Pastor Harry so he can correct me if he thinks I have written anything that is unreasonable or unloving. I invite you to discuss it with your parents if you wish. I continue to pray earnestly for you, as I do for your wife and children.

Yours in the love that Christ alone can give,

Martin

About Day One:

Day One's threefold commitment:

•To be faithful to the Bible, God's inerrant, infallible Word;
•To be relevant to our modern generation;
•To be excellent in our publication standards.

I continue to be thankful for the publications of Day One. They are biblical; they have sound theology; and they are relative to the issues at hand. The material is condensed and manageable while, at the same time, being complete—a challenging balance to find. We are happy in our ministry to make use of these excellent publications.

JOHN MACARTHUR, PASTOR-TEACHER, GRACE COMMUNITY CHURCH, CALIFORNIA

It is a great encouragement to see Day One making such excellent progress. Their publications are always biblical, accessible and attractively produced, with no compromise on quality. Long may their progress continue and increase!

JOHN BLANCHARD, AUTHOR, EVANGELIST AND APOLOGIST

Visit our website for more information and to request a free catalogue of our books.

www.dayone.co.uk

No Longer Two

BRIAN AND BARBARA EDWARDS

ISBN 978–1–84625–173–3

192 PAGES, PAPERBACK

No Longer Two is a workbook for couples preparing for marriage. Designed in a contemporary and accessible style, it faces the issues that will confront two people committing the whole of their lives together. With Preparation questions and a short, relevant Bible Study for each chapter, it is especially designed for all who take seriously God's revealed plan for marriage.

No Longer Two has become a standard workbook used by church leaders in many countries for the vital ministry of preparing a man and a woman for the most exciting and challenging adventure of their lives.

ages understand biblical teaching on these matters and why fidelity to God's vision for men and women in his world is so vital.'
MICHAEL HAYKIN, NORTH AMERICA

'Quite simply one of the best books on the market today on the subject of marriage'
THE MONTHLY RECORD, SCOTLAND

'We bought Brian and Barbara Edwards' book two years after we were married and found that its practical problem-solving strategies and insightful candidness made us wish we'd had it right from the beginning!'
MARKO AND MIRIAM, AUSTRALIA

'It is written in a warm, clear style. It is thoroughly biblical, and eminently practical and pastoral ... excellent treatment of such a vital topic.'
EVANGELICAL TIMES, ENGLAND

'A keen student of both Scripture and Western culture, Brian helps Christians of all

BRIAN STONE

ISBN 978–1–84625–129–0

128 PAGES, PAPERBACK

This book is the end result of a family effort. The use of catechisms and confessions has been an invaluable help and tool to us in our family devotions. Over an extended period of time, as we have worked through the Westminster Shorter Catechism, we have taken the liberty of rephrasing the questions and answers, not only into modern English, but also at the same time endeavouring to add a Baptist understanding to the questions on baptism.

Questions have been added where we felt the need for further understanding and application. Talking points have been added to encourage further thought and discussion on the questions. The Scriptural references, which you are encouraged to read, have, by and large, been taken from other catechisms, and they are essential to an understanding of the truth.

The purpose of this current revision is to encourage Christian families in their family devotions with the aid of this Catechism. The talking points are there to stimulate discussion and to see what the level of understanding is among your children.

Bible readings have been added which will take you through the Scriptures, in a Scripture reading plan. These readings are not related to the questions and answers.

Reference to hymns is made throughout, as the use of these always helps to embed an understanding of the truth in the head as well as drive it into the heart.

'It is obvious that a man must always know, about any given subject, a great deal more than he is going to teach. Brian Stone has proved the benefits and blessings of teaching children Christian truths and values in family worship by means of the Catechism. This book will be a great aid for those whose aim it is to make family worship enjoyable and profitable. From our own personal experience my wife and I have found that teaching children by means of the Children's Catechism has been invaluable, and I am glad to see this publication being made available at this time.'

WILLIAM G. HUGHES PASTOR, EMMANUEL BAPTIST CHURCH, COCONUT CREEK, FLORIDA, USA

Lead your family in worship

FRANCOIS CARR

ISBN: 978-1-84625-128-3

80 PAGES, PAPERBACK

All churches want to experience growth. Many churches are implementing special projects and techniques in order to achieve this growth. But churches consist of families—and families consist of individuals. If a family is spiritually healthy, it leads to spontaneous growth in the church and to the spiritual development of the community. Yet few churches focus their growth, particularly their spiritual growth, on the foundation of the holiness of individuals and family members. The traditional practice of family worship has become neglected as a result.

Here Francois Carr pleads for the return of family worship times. What is family worship? Why is it so rarely practised today? What should a family worship time consist of? How can my family get started? Illustrated with examples of many great men and women in church history, this book answers these questions and demonstrates the influence for good that the practice of family worship has had down through the centuries. Appendixes are included to examples family worship sessions in action.

Francois Carr, B. Th., M.C.C., D. Min., NDPB, is currently the Executive Director both of Revival South Africa and Te Deum Ministries. He is the senior editor of Revival, A Journal On Prayer, Holiness and Revival. He is co-sponsor of the Heart Cry Conferences in the USA, Malawi

Francois Carr

and South Africa. He is also the author of several books and a popular conference speaker in the USA, UK, Europe and several countries in Africa. Francois is married to Dorothea and they have one daughter, Leoné.

'Anyone who knows Francois Carr quickly recognizes two things: he has a heart for his family and he longs for revival. In this helpful work, Francois combines the two. A heart for God is learned at home. Holiness is taught at home. If there is to be revival in our land and if there are to be great men and women of God leading our churches, then Christian parents must take seriously their calling to raise up a godly generation in their homes. This helpful work will be a great help to those parents seeking to build homes that honor God.'
DR RICHARD BLACKABY, DIRECTOR OF BLACKABY MINISTRIES, CANADA

God's prescription

ANDREW OLIVER

ISBN: 978–1–84625–095–8

160 PAGES, PAPERBACK

God's prescription
For a healthy marriage and family

Andrew Oliver   Day One

The family is under threat. Contemporary culture and changes in legislation are seeking to redefine its structure, parents are increasingly giving over to the state the responsibility of disciplining their children, and homes are constantly bombarded by immoral images of the 'family' through TV. The great need today is to return to biblical principles for family life. The Bible is God's manual for the people he created in his image, and therefore it has much to say on this crucial issue. Here, Andy Oliver guides us helpfully through the biblical teaching on marriage and family life, and emphasizes the need to follow God's Word if we are to build solid foundations for a healthy family.

You will benefit greatly from this refreshingly direct and practical introduction to what the Bible teaches.
JONATHAN LAMB, AUTHOR, DIRECTOR OF LANGHAM PREACHING (LANGHAM PARTNERSHIP INTERNATIONAL) AND FORMER ASSOCIATE GENERAL SECRETARY OF IFES, UK